THE WRINKLIES' BEDSIDE COMPANION

First published in Great Britain in 2010

Prion Books
an imprint of the
Carlton Publishing Group
20 Mortimer Street
London W1T 3JW

A catalogue record for this book is available from the British Library

ISBN 978-1-85375-784-6

Printed in the UK by CPI Mackays, Chatham, ME5 8TD

10 9 8 7 6 5 4 3

THE WRINKLIES' BEDSIDE COMPANION

How To Drop Off Before Anything Else Drops Off

Mike Haskins &
Clive Whichelow

PRION

Contents

Introduction

Now why would a wrinkly need another bedside companion? You already have your hot water bottle, your bedside drink, the book that you read a page and a half of before nodding off, and all your other bedtime bits and bobs. Not to mention your long-suffering wrinkly other half.

Ah, but this is something else. This is something to tickle your fancy, tickle your ribs and let you luxuriate in the joys of being a wrinkly.

Inside these pages you will find everything you need to know to help you sleep like a baby. A rather wrinkled baby, naturally, but where else would you find the meaning of wrinkly dreams, the definitive list of wrinkly bedtime essentials or even wrinkly prayers?

With the aid of this book you can delve into the history of sleep with Rip Van Wrinkly, run through the town in your nightgown with Wee Willie Wrinkly, or sing yourself to sleep with 'Wrinkly The Best'.

Or perhaps you could rearrange your bedroom for the ultimate sleep experience with your very own version of Feng Shui, plan your superannuated bedtime snacks with your very own menu du wrinkly or compose letters of complaint to all those companies, organisations, and thoughtless individuals who have upset you today.

You could marvel at the achievements of other people well into wrinkliehood, find out surefire cures for wrinkly insomnia, and look out for the tell-tale signs of things that might go wrinkly in the night.

Your bed is your final sanctuary after another day out there in the frankly confusing modern world. The world of blogs and tweets, bogofs, Asbos, and reality TV; the world of speed dialling, speed dating, laptops, Blackberries, iPhones, iPods, YouTube, Facebook, self-service tills, online banking, downloading, upspeaking, and celebrities you've never heard of; the world of sub-prime, super-sizing and global warming, and all those other mind-boggling things that have been put on this Earth to bewilder and befuddle your grizzled grey matter in the Autumn of your years.

But help is at hand!

Here in this book you will find positive thoughts for grumpy wrinklies (yes, there are some, believe it or not), tips on getting a good night's sleep (without the aid of half the contents of your medical cabinet), and even a few sartorial pointers as to what the fashion-conscious wrinkly should be considering for his or her bedtime attire (anything described in your favourite mail-order catalogue as 'skimpy' will not be appropriate).

There are a thousand and one books out there about the meaning of dreams, but how many are there which interpret the nocturnal nightmares and three o'clock fantasies of the not-so-young-at-heart?

None, until now.

The dreams of the everyday wrinkly cannot be compared to those of the thrusting young things of the Twitterati. No, wrinkly dreams are something else altogether and need to be considered and analysed as a separate phenomenon in their own right.

Bedtime for wrinkies should not merely be considered a time to sleep, perchance to dream. It should be an experience, a joy, something to be looked forward to. This means making sure you have all your bedtime essentials close to hand when you retire for the night.

This enlightening book will provide a handy list of bedside can't-do-withouts to help you to ease your way through the night.

And when you wake up at 4 o'clock in a cold sweat worrying about this, that or the other, then reach for your handy bedside companion to comfort, console and cosset you through the wee small hours.

It'll be just like having a hot water bottle that never goes cold, a nightcap that never needs topping up, or a partner who stays mercifully quiet while you have a good old grumble.

This jolly tome is there for every circumstance, whether you imagine you hear something going bump in the night, fancy that you can see a ghostly spectre hovering at the end of the bed or worry that you're warming your feet on the cat and have actually put the hot water bottle out the back door for the night by mistake.

In the long hours of sleeplessness you will find lists of inventions that wrinkles like your good self are waiting for, stories that you look forward to reading in the news when your morning paper plops onto the doormat, plus of course, the wrinkles' guide to insomnia.

It's not called a companion for nothing. It's there for you when no one else is and even your partner is snoring like a baby. It's handy at bedtime with its wrinkly bedtime check list, and it's handy in the morning when you get up, look in the mirror and need to read the section on How to Look Good Wrinkly. It's also there in between with lists of ideas on how to while away the hours when you just can't quite manage to drop off.

In short, it's the answer to your wrinkly bedtime prayers. It also contains a bit of blue sky wrinkly thinking such as: what if the entire world were peopled exclusively by wrinklies? You may think that it is already the case if you live in a retirement home, a gated community or certain parts of the south coast, but, in the words of the song, what a wonderful world this would be…

Yes, whatever the eventuality, you will find the answer here in these pages. It will even answer questions you never thought, or never dared, to ask.

An oracle, a treasure trove, an almanac and a bedtime snack tray all rolled into one. How did you ever manage without one?

So, stop worrying, lie back and forget all about it.

Say it loud, you're Wrinkly and you're proud!

Chapter 1: So You've Survived Another Day Then!

There's a certain point in your wrinkly life when you see each day not just as a new challenge, but also as a personal achievement in actually getting through it and living to tell the tale.

And frankly, when you look at all the things a wrinkly has to contend with it's up there with Sir Edmund Hillary climbing Everest, Buzz Aldrin going on his zero-gravity walkabout on the moon, or Eddie 'the Eagle' Edwards being taken even slightly seriously as a contender in the Winter Olympics.

Up to around middle age your body performs well enough for you not to even have to think about it most of the time.

You take it for granted that you can get from A to B without the aid of an oxygen mask, that you can eat a bag of nuts without worrying what it's going to do to your teeth, or to be able to read a road map without holding it at arm's length outside the car.

Eventually you reach what's known in medical circles as 'the Dalek years' when you can no longer get up the stairs.

Bit by wobbly bit the wheels start falling off your bus.

Little bits of sight, little bits of hearing, mobility and grey matter fall by the wayside until you're like one of those mechanical monkeys that didn't have the long-life batteries installed, and you come to a shuddering halt.

So, to actually survive another day with these handicaps is quite an achievement in itself.

Of course, all these things aren't irritants to wrinklies exclusively, but it is the wrinkly who suffers most because the wrinkly grew up in a different world. A world of good manners, customer service and politeness.

Youngsters don't know any better. They expect people to be walking around wired up like robots to phones, iPods, laptops, pedometers, and all the rest of it.

They expect to have to bleep their own groceries, and remember their chip and pin numbers. They expect to have their picture taken by CCTV every 20 seconds and to have their bags checked when they visit a museum, or to have to put their rubbish in 15 different coloured bins no more than a foot from their front gate.

They have never known roads without humps that almost jolt your teeth into your lap every time you go over them. In short, they don't know how much nicer it all used to be.

But the wrinkly does; and it is for this reason that every day survived in the mad, bad and dangerous modern world is a personal triumph, a great achievement, an accolade-worthy, spine-tingling, air-punching success in the teeth of the mightiest foes the modern world can throw at them.

Probably just how Sir Edmund Hillary felt in fact.

Well done, wrinklies everywhere!

Ten Things A Wrinkly Needs To Survive The Day

1. A sense of humour

If you can't take a joke you shouldn't have joined the wrinkly army. So it's probably best to join in with everyone else and start enjoying a good old chuckle at yourself. After all from now on you are going to have practical jokes played on you every single day by your own body.

2. A sense of the ridiculous

Come on! Surely you can't still believe that life is ever going to make much sense. That's as bad as presuming that the people around you are going to behave sensibly or that it will ever be possible to elect a government that looks like it knows what it's doing. Surely you're not clinging onto these naïve delusions! Not after you've lived this long! Besides doesn't the daily hunt for reading glasses that are dangling from a string round your neck require a certain attitude de l'absurd?

3. Someone else who can remember 'the good old days'

Charming as some young people can be, there's not much point in discussing the past with them. There's nothing quite like a stroll down memory lane with someone of your own vintage to the times when shop assistants called you 'sir' or 'madam', when policemen were reassuringly middle-aged, and when you could phone any company in the UK and complain in person to a real, live human being – ah, bliss!

4. Those little home comforts

Imagine your worst nightmares: a traffic jam with tattooed lorry drivers swearing and gesticulating at you just because you are blocking 'their' lane, or a clothes shop where all the assistants seem to be about 15 years old and the clothes seem to be made for Twiggy's thinner young sister. Now imagine your comfy armchair, TV remote at your fingertips, the kettle boiling gently in the background, a nice piece of cake, and your battered old slippers. No contest really is it?

5. A good strong drink

The good news is that it's far too late to do you much harm now. And besides, you're so shaky on your pins people probably think you're half cut most of the time anyway.

6. At least two pairs of glasses

There's your main pair, of course; then there are your reading glasses, your 'spare' pair, your 'old' sellotaped pair for emergencies, possibly a tinted pair that you bought in a moment of madness or got in a 'buy one, get one free' offer, your driving glasses...

7. Some proper food

We all like a curry now and again, but for goodness sake, is it necessary for every pub and restaurant the length and breadth of Britain to be serving foreign food all the time? What exactly is a fajita anyway?

8. A bit of peace and quiet

Why people can't get through the day without that 'boom boom boom' racket going on – or why TV shows can't go two seconds without background music, or radio traffic reports can't be delivered without some ghastly 'rock' music playing in the background – is anybody's guess. And don't even get me started on road drills, personal stereos, shop muzak, ice cream vans...

9. A nice cup of tea

It's what the British Empire was built on.

10. A good old moan

Forget all your yoga, feng shui, Pilates, Indian head massages, body waxing, colonic irrigation, tanning salons, hot tubs and all that other old nonsense. There's nothing like a good moan to cleanse the system and put life back in the old wrinkly.

Positive Thoughts For Grumpy Wrinklies At The End Of A Long Hard Day

- If nobody complained nothing would ever get any better
- I'm not as miserable as that old bloke/old biddy next door
- I'm past the stage where I need to worry about what I eat
- I don't understand modern art, and frankly I'm quite glad
- My life insurance seems to be getting so much cheaper these days
- I'm beyond fashion
- The best tunes are played on the oldest violins
- If experience comes with age I should probably be running the country by now
- I drink, therefore I am
- The older you get, the more memories you have – well, at least, if you can remember them
- Fewer and fewer people can remember all the things I did wrong when I was younger
- OK, I go to more funerals these days, but at least they're not my own

The Obstacles You've Overcome Today

The average wrinkly has seen a great many changes in his or her lifetime. When you're young you take these in your stride. As the advancing years take their toll however you begin to find these continual changes unnecessary, excessive and, not to put to fine a point on it, a bit of a pain in the wrinkled old posterior.

Anyone would think that there is someone out there whose entire existence is spent in dreaming up annoying little changes to hamper your smooth progress through the day.

Let's call him Mr Scroggins!

Shopping

Shopping used to be so simple: you went to a shop, told the shop assistant what you wanted, handed over the cash (and it usually was cash), and they handed you your purchase and your change.

Then Mr Scroggins decreed that, oh no, that's far too simple! From this day forth you will be issued with a trolley at the supermarket and have to collect all your groceries yourself!

Then, because supermarket trolleys were being commandeered by local yobbos and being used as impromptu art installations in local ponds and rivers, Mr Scroggins decided that from now on you would have to pay a deposit of £1 before you could get your trolley. So, on arrival at the supermarket you probably have to make sure you've got some small change (or, more likely, some quite large change) for the car park, and a pound coin for the trolley.

For a few years all went smoothly (apart from the odd dodgy trolley wheel) until Mr Scroggins decided that what we all needed was loyalty cards.

So, not only do you have to remember your car park money, and your pound coin for the trolley, you also have to remember your loyalty card.

This is bad enough for people with quite good memories, but no so brilliant for people whose memories are not 100% reliable. Oh, and nowadays of course, you have to remember your chip and pin as well.

Then, with his green hat on, Mr Scroggins announced that you should start remembering to bring your own shopping bags to the supermarket. Hot on the heels of this little gem was turning the customer into his or her own cashier! That's right, bleeping your own bleeping groceries through the bleeper if you please! And then afterwards faffing around with the payment machine instead of having the cashier do it for you!

And has anyone ever managed to use one of these self service machines without it eventually getting confused and summoning the assistant to sort out the 'unexpected item' it has detected in the bagging area?

If this self-service lark goes any further they may as well just issue you with your own set of keys to the supermarket so you can go and help yourself whenever you want to. You'll probably be expected to mop the floor once in a while as well and chase shoplifters.

Happy shopping!

Driving

Another of life's little pleasures made a misery by jobsworths of all descriptions.

Do you realize that at one time you didn't even have to pass a test to be able to drive a car?

They soon put a stop to that!

Then came traffic lights, breath tests, yellow lines, traffic wardens, bollards, width restrictors, chicanes, speed limits, sleeping policemen, photo ID, penalty points, motorway hazard warnings – or sometimes just little bits of useful advice such as 'tiredness kills', or 'don't forget to breathe' – controlled parking zones, wheel clamps, bus lanes, and a thousand and one other petty annoyances that should make you want to never set foot in a car again, but actually increase your resolve to beat the system.

If you tried to read all the signs they put at the side of the road, you'd have no time left to watch the cars around you. And of course to read the signs at your age you have to constantly swap between your distance and reading glasses. All this just to drive round the corner to the shops!

Apart from the official interference, you also have to put up with other road users who are rude, inconsiderate or just plain daft.

Whether it's Lycra louts weaving their bikes in and out of the traffic, lorry drivers changing lanes without signalling, taxis stopping abruptly, or buses forming an unpassable convoy it's enough to leave you blubbing like a baby.

And who was the genius who invented the traffic lights that stay on green for five minutes as you're driving towards them only to then change at the very last moment? Why not just have done with it and have the message 'Ha ha! Got you again, sucker!' flash up over the red light?

Then there are the squeegee merchants who give your windscreen the once over while you're stuck at the lights. For one scary moment, as you see a massive white splodge suddenly appear on your windscreen, you imagine you have been targeted by a passing albatross.

Then you have charity collectors dressed as giant rabbits or something rattling buckets of money at you while you sit fuming in an interminable line of traffic, or people who stuff leaflets under your windscreen wipers the moment you've parked.

We should look on the bright side however. Our roads should all be in perfect condition by now. After all they seem to keep digging them up every time you leave the house.

The simple act of climbing into your car is like walking through a wardrobe into a Narnia of nonsense, annoyance, irritation and hassle.

What on earth would Henry Ford have made of it all? He probably thought the car would mean freedom for all. He said a man would 'enjoy with his family the blessing of hours of pleasure in God's great open spaces.' He obviously hadn't envisaged the M25 on a bank holiday weekend.

Walking

You would have thought walking would have been one of those things that came as naturally as night following day.

Try walking down a busy town high street though and it's a different matter altogether. If you can manage to go more than about 20 yards (oh, all right, metres if you must) without being accosted by a market researcher, a charity collector or a *Big Issue* seller then you're lucky indeed.

How did companies manage before they hit upon the idea of market 'ree-search' as its proponents insist on pronouncing it?

When Mr Coca and Mr Cola started their famous brand, they probably just had a hunch people might like it.

Same for Mr Heinz. He probably didn't mess around with market ree-search, he just jumped in feet first and launched 57 varieties. Good on him.

Then there are the charity collectors. Once upon a time you'd just pop your threepenny bit into the tin, collect your little flag and wear it with pride for the rest of the day. Whatever happened to those little flags by the way? Apart from anything else it protected you from being accosted by another charity collector five yards up the road.

These days, they don't want your threepenny bits or the modern equivalents anymore. They want you to sign up to have considerable sums removed from your bank account by direct debit every month. It's not for nothing these people are called 'chuggers', or charity muggers.

And then you have to contend with your fellow pedestrians constantly getting in your way. They seem oblivious to everything and everyone around them. Clearly the reason they're on foot is because if they were ever allowed behind the wheel of a car, a mass pile up would result as soon as they pulled out from their driveway.

Apart from these hazards in human form, we wrinklies also have to contend with loose paving stones, little green men at crossings that turn red before you can get halfway across the road, dropped chewing gum, banana skins, cars driving by with some dreadful rap music blaring out of the open windows, scary-looking people with shaven heads, tattoos, hoodies, and bits of metal sticking out of their faces, and people constantly yabbering away on mobile phones.

Add to this those geriatrics speeding down the pavement in their motorised scooters re-enacting the chariot scenes in Ben Hur, and a myriad other nuisances and it's a wonder any of us wrinklies are still around to tell the tale.

Around the house

Did you know that most accidents occur in the home? Apparently, eleven people every year die putting their trousers on. We can probably assume that a similar number die in the process of taking them off.

Not only do we feel terrified whenever we leave the house, clearly we should be terrified when we get home again as well!

Yes, never mind the mean streets, just getting down to the breakfast table can be fraught with danger for wrinklies.

You know what it's like, the alarm clock blasting down your ear almost gives you a heart attack. You lie there for a few moments until the terrible realisation hits you: you're still alive so you have to get up after all.

You drag yourself out of bed but haven't yet put your glasses on so you step on the cat at the top of the stairs. If the physical obstruction itself isn't enough to send you flying down the apples and pears at breakneck speed then the sound of your moggie making an ear-splitting yowl will be enough to bring on a cardiac arrest.

When you get to the breakfast table sans specs you need to be doubly vigilant that you are pouring cereal into your breakfast bowl and not the cat's crunchy treats.

Also, without your bifocals it may be difficult to read the small print warning that your breakfast may contain nuts, or that it has more E numbers than a 1967 vintage car rally.

Then you have to check the salt content and the sugar content, and make sure you're not putting that wicked full cream milk on it – heavens no, you might actually enjoy it!

Yes, whatever you do, don't forget that anything that makes life worth living will probably kill you. So in order to keep healthy, avoid anything enjoyable. Then not only will you live longer, it will seem longer as well!

OK, so you survived breakfast, now you've got to deal with all those flipping nuisances who knock on the door uninvited. Double glazing salesmen, Jehovah's Witnesses (what happens when a double glazing salesman calls at a Jehovah's Witness's house or vice versa?), charity collectors, jumble collectors, postmen with parcels for next door, people selling fresh fish or manure or some such thing, meter readers, people who can't tell Acacia Avenue from Acacia Close, children playing 'knock down ginger', people who want to prune your trees or fix your roof or pave your drive.

You begin to see why the rich employ butlers.

If they're not ringing your doorbell, they're ringing your phone. Cold-calling salesmen, wrong numbers, people doing surveys, people who hang up as soon as you pick up the phone, and those really irritating people who demand 'who's that?' when they've phoned you!

Yet, despite what life in your own home throws at you, you've survived another day. OK, you've been driven to distraction at times, but as you lay down your head to sleep you can feel quietly proud of yourself.

Things Your Body Is Trying To Tell You

Aching joints

You're trying to do too much. Lifting a cup of tea and working the remote control with the same hand all the time is going to lead to all sorts of problems, so alternate hands or get someone else to change channels.

Feeling tired all the time

You've not been having your afternoon nap have you?

Why do you think they made daytime TV so boring?

Yes, precisely – so you will nod off and catch up on your beauty sleep.

You don't think you're actually supposed to watch Weakest Antique Celebrity Bargain Deal House Cash Garden Makeover Roadshow Revisited do you?

Ringing in your ears

You've gone to sleep with the phone under the pillow again.

Forgetfulness

You're now at the age where you don't much fancy remembering exactly how old you are so your memory is starting to block out these unwelcome bits of information.

Listlessness

Your blood sugar levels are low. You should be eating more biccies, drinking more hot sweet tea and having regular slabs of cake.

The weight gain may even help to smooth out some of those wrinkles!

Blurred vision

Having a bottle or two of what you fancy around the house, or maybe even your very own fully-functioning bar with optics, beer mats, ice buckets et al constantly on hand is, to say the least, a bit of a temptation.

If the blurred vision isn't a sign of deteriorating eyesight then it may just be the constant gush of alcohol in your front room. It is probably no coincidence that 'cataract' is also another word for 'waterfall'.

Loss of balance

See above.

Back pain

Starting your TV viewing at 9am and ending when you drop off in front of the late night film could be a contributory factor. Either that, or it's the constant offers of 'buy one, get one free' that entice you to lug home twice as much you actually want from the supermarket.

Wrinklies Vs The Awkward Squad

Who are the Awkward Squad? The rest of the non-wrinkly world basically.

You're probably old enough to remember going to the shops and being served by a shop assistant. Then the supermarkets took over and you had to go round getting your own groceries and packing them yourself.

How long will it be before they expect you to dig your own potatoes out of the ground and climb up a tree in the supermarket car park to get your own apples too? Progress? Schmogress!

Even when you park your car you need the brain of Stephen Hawking to remember where you left it in some vast multi-storey car park.

This is all very well for people in the prime of life with grey cells to spare, but we wrinklies need our little grey cells for more important things such as remembering when Corrie starts (unless it's been moved again because of the flipping football) or how to work the microwave.

Yes, the big wide world out there is anti-wrinkly. We have laws against ageism, so that yes, seventy-five year-olds can apply to be nightclub bouncers if they really want to, but it's the little things that make life difficult. For example, why do they print instructions so small? You get your medicine home from the chemist's and inside is a leaflet folded up half a dozen times and which opens out into something the size of a judo mat.

At the top, in large letters, it says 'read carefully before starting treatment.' The rest is printed in type that could fit the entire contents of the Bible onto the back of a postage stamp.

This is not helpful for the average wrinkly, especially if the medicine in question is the eye drops without which you can see virtually nothing anyway.

You used to have a phone in the hall and that was that. Now you have to be available '24/7' on your mobile. Some people are so attached to their mobiles that they have a thing permanently clipped to their ear, making them look like a tagged dairy cow.

Even if you don't want a mobile you're virtually forced to have one because everyone else expects you to have one. Then there's the inter-bloody-net.

Want to go somewhere? The cinema maybe, a tourist attraction? You have to book online. No more of that simply turning up and buying a ticket. You have to go through more menus than Egon Ronay before you can do anything these days. And people are always telling you to 'check out our website.' Why?

It's as though all organisations want to keep you at arm's length while they continue with the important business of relieving you of your hard-earned cash.

Even if you phone the police to complain about the little yobbos graffitiing your fence you get put through to a call centre miles away. Typical!

The Awkward Squad – watch out, they're everywhere!

More Positive Thoughts For Grumpy Wrinklies At The End Of A Long Hard Day

- I'll probably get an MBE for moaning
- When my children have children it will be a rather delicious sort of poetic justice
- It don't mean a thing if it ain't got that whinge
- If God had meant me to climb stairs he wouldn't have invented the stairlift would he now?
- I'll never have to join a social networking site on the internet
- I don't care what my ring-tone sounds like or whether it's cool
- In some cultures I would be venerated as an elder statesperson
- I enjoy telling people the same old stories over and over again because my memory's so bad that I'm always quite surprised to hear the ending even though it's me that's saying it
- For the first time in my life I am a bit of a character thanks to the combination of senility, out of date opinions and 15 different tablets my doctor has prescribed for me each day
- People are still making all the same stupid mistakes I've seen my entire life. Now I can just sit back and enjoy watching them do it
- Doddering is better than actually falling over
- I'm old enough to know better but forgetful enough not to care
- If I were a wine, I'd be called vintage

- If I were an outfit of clothes or a car I'd be called a classic
- If I were a building, I'd be listed and have a preservation order slapped on me
- If I were some kind of mechanical object the same age as myself, a group of enthusiasts would be giving up their time to restore me to perfect working order
- I have to be given free access to public transport now because of the danger I'd pose if I tried to drive myself anywhere
- If every wrinkle is a laughter line then I must have brought joy and happiness to the world!
- If life is a bowl of cherries who gets the pits?
- Age before beauty? Does that mean I've still got the beauty to come?
- I should soon be of an age when I'll be preserved for posterity by the National Trust
- I'm still 21 on the inside!

Chapter 2:
The W Factor

In our youth-obsessed culture it's easy to forget that wrinklies rule the world. OK, we've got a few fresh-faced British politicians strutting their stuff on the world stage, but look at the woman who has the power to tell them when they can form a government.

Not that we'd dream of branding the Queen a wrinkly, but she is in her 80s remember and has seen off a dozen or so of these thrusting young Prime Ministers over the years.

Have you ever seen a young Pope? Exactly.

And who's that bloke who always puts the fear of God into stock markets the world over? Alan Greenspan. He was still Chairman of the Federal Reserve when he was 80. And the other one, what's his name? Warren Buffett, aka the Sage of Omaha (1930 vintage). Even relative whippersnapper Bill Gates is the wrong side of 50.

Sexiest man in the world? Sean Connery (born 1930). Sexiest woman? Dame Helen Mirren (born 1945). Greatest artist who ever lived? Pablo Picasso – still dipping his brush well into his eighties.

You're getting the picture now? Yes, young people can do all that supermodel/footballer stuff, and good luck to them, but all the important stuff is in the hands of wrinklies.

Ever heard of the Illuminati? It's a shadowy secret society of people who really run the world. Forget all your presidents and prime ministers and all that; these are the people who are really pulling the strings.

And you know what? They're all wrinklies.

Yes, the hands of power have liver spots on them. The Wrinkleati, as we should probably be calling them, have the entire future of mankind in their rheumatic grip. And so it should be.

Modern societies have got it all frack to bunt. They've let these youngsters clamber to the top of the greasy pole while they're still wet behind the whatsits – if that's not mixing our metaphors too much.

The ancients got it right. Tribal elders. You never hear of any proper civilizations being built by tribal youngers do you? And there's a very good reason for that. Wrinklies are better at everything. All the important stuff anyway.

When some buffoon goes and bankrupts his bank by dodgy dealing it's always someone who looks like he hasn't started shaving yet.

When you go on a spiritual journey to seek some yogi living in a cave who is supposed to have the meaning of life at his fingertips you don't want to be greeted by a teenager in a pair of jeans and a Ché Guevara T-shirt do you?

When you finally receive your long-deserved knighthood or damehood you don't want to get it from some junior member of the royal family who's just got back from a night's clubbing, you want to be tapped on the shoulder by someone with more lines on their face than you've got. Dignity. Gravitas. Seniority. Stuff like that. In other words, The W factor.

How To Be A Wrinkly

People think it's easy, but it so isn't – as your younger family members might say.

They think it's simply a case of getting older. Just start young and let Mother Nature do the rest. No, being a wrinkly is as much a state of mind as it is the state of your body. For example:

Dress

The accent is on comfort. No more tottering around in high heels or showing off hectares of bare flesh. Especially if you're a bloke.

Interests

You've had all the excitement you need in your youth thank you very much, so now it's time for a bit of dull. You should now be getting up at around the same time as you used to go to bed as a teenager.

Friends

Friends are people you share interests with, but true friends are people who never remind you how old you are. Probably because they're the same age. It's a sort of unwritten wrinkly pact.

Outlook

When you grow out of the challenges of family, job, etc you have to invent new challenges. Being able to stay awake through an entire film at the cinema for example, or being able to crouch down to pick something up and then stand again without holding onto anything.

Role

As it is the teenager's role in life to be a flaming nuisance, so it is the wrinkly's role to disapprove. The wrinkly's disapproval does not of course have to confine itself to teenagers, it can include: declining standards of broadcasting, almost any change or modernisation, and the tops of medicine bottles being impossible to unscrew.

History

A wrinkly does not fully live in the present. Perhaps three quarters of a wrinkly's existence is spent in an imaginary golden past where young people were polite and respectful, where you didn't have to choose between 170 TV channels, when smoking wasn't harmful and beer was tuppence a pint.

The star of this vintage newsreel is our wrinkly, who as a younger person was a model child, a sensible teenager, and an industrious young adult who could work out the cost of 27 aniseed balls at a farthing a half dozen without the aid of a calculator.

Tastes

Music: not too loud; food: not too spicy; decor: not too bright (or dark); company: not too long.

Exercise

Exercise must be entirely incidental. None of this 'going to the gym' nonsense. Put biscuits on top shelf in kitchen for stretching exercises. Walking to kitchen for biscuits is about as cardio-vascular as you want to get at your time of life. Lifting your own body weight out of the armchair to walk to kitchen is weight training in anyone's book. Sorted.

If The World Was Entirely Peopled By Wrinklies...

What a wonderful world it would be! Yes, Sir Harry Secombe should have sung a song about it. If we ruled the world, every day would be pension payout day, every day would be free of horrible booming music, every day would be full of people being polite to one another. OK, it doesn't quite scan as well as Sir Harry's version, but the sentiment's there.

Too much in the world today is centred around young people and what they want. Yes, we were all young once (though we're pretty sure we didn't get up to half what the youngsters today get up to), but the fact is that the majority of the population are over 40. Over 80% of the cash in the UK is in the hands of the over 50s (where's my share then, we hear you ask).

So, if we just take this a smidgeon further to an imaginary world entirely peopled by wrinklies we'd have:

- No more burglary (the average age of a burglar is 16 to 24 – bring back national service at once!)
- No more boy racers on the roads.
- No more 24-hour drinking, late night partying, and general din.
- Lovely quiet pubs without big screens, thumping music and young bar staff who don't know a gin and it from an egg nog.
- Proper queues at bus stops instead of a brawling rabble of foul-mouthed schoolchildren.
- Decent radio stations with proper music.
- Nice TV shows without swearing.

- No more dreadful offspring of celebrities in the paper all the time or so-called supermodels, footballers, daft pop stars, etc.
- People talking properly instead of in this ghastly yoofspeak.
- Proper clothes shops with suits and dresses and other smart attire (jeans may be all right for doing the gardening in, but...)
- Restaurants where you can order a sandwich without having to choose between submarines, wraps, ciabattas, baguettes, and all those other bizarre concoctions.

Of course, there may be some drawbacks to a world entirely people by wrinklies. For instance:

- The pin-ups in the paper might not be quite so alluring.
- Would you want your laser eye surgery to be performed by someone whose hands were shaking?
- The Olympics could be a bit dull.
- The bin men would be even slower.
- Our overseas fighting forces would be like *Dad's Army* (without Pike).
- YMCA would have to change its name to the WMCA.
- The Rolling Stones would be considered a boy band again.
- Who would you get to sort out your computer problems?
- There'd be no more toyboys or dollybirds available when you won the lottery.
- Who could you blame the state of the world on?

Real-Life Wrinkly Achievements

Never, in the field of human achievement, has so much been done by so many wrinklies. Sorry, Winston, for paraphrasing one of your greatest speeches, but it neatly sums up what it is to be a wrinkly today.

Once upon a time, you were over the hill at 40, on the scrapheap at 50, and virtually invisible by the age of 60. Once you'd reached retirement you were expected to eke out your last days in an armchair on a diet of tea and biccies and listening to *Mrs Dale's Diary* on the wireless. Not now though – we've got daytime TV!

No, all joking aside, the modern wrinkly is a force of nature – hang gliding, windsurfing, marathon running, writing novels, climbing mountains, swimming with dolphins, learning Chinese, mastering the Internet... quite a busy weekend all in all.

And famous wrinklies don't retire or give up. They just carry on doing what they've always done, but slightly slower.

Rock & Roll

Take the Rolling Stones. Between 2007 and 2009 their Bigger Bang tour grossed over half a billion(!) dollars, the biggest in history. At the time the combined age of the band was around 4,002 (allegedly).

Sex Symbols

Even famous beauties just carry on regardless – Sophia Loren (born 1934) can still show these young bimbos a thing or two, and Joan Collins (one year older than La Loren), and Honor Blackman (another eight years older than Joanie, but who's counting?) can still set the pulses of men racing. Though for wrinkly men that can of course be rather dangerous.

And the women still seem to like the cut of the jib of blokes like Clint Eastwood and Sean Connery (both born 1930), Michael Caine (1933) and Robert Redford (1936).

The fact that they also have quite a lot of money of course is absolutely nothing to do with it, all you cynics out there!

Arts, Fashion, etc

Michaelangelo was still working on churches in his eighties, Pablo Picasso was still painting at the same age, Coco Chanel was still running her fashion empire as an octogenarian, and at around the same age Pablo Casales was playing cello concertos… It just goes to show, if you've got an 'o' at the end of your name it's a passport to longevity.

Mind you, if your name's George you're in with a chance too. Playwright George Bernard Shaw was still writing in his nineties, actor George Burns worked until he was almost a hundred, and King George II was still going into battle at the age of 60 which, taking age inflation into account, is probably about 102.

Inventions

In 1996 at the grand old age of 59 Trevor Baylis won the BBC Design Award for his invention, the clockwork radio. People thought it was a wind-up, and it was, but in rather a good way.

In 2010 'veteran' 'renegade' (fill in your own epithet) ex-MP Tony Benn revealed that at the age of 85 he had invented the 'seatcase', a sort of suitcase that incorporates a nifty chair for people who need to sit around en route. Was it a coincidence that it was announced in the middle of a BA strike? With wrinklies in mind though, how about a 'loocase'? Just a suggestion...

Showbiz

From Tony Benn to Tony Bennett (was he originally known as Anthony Wedgwood Bennett we wonder?) Of 1926 vintage the Bennster is still singing, painting, and variously not giving a fig about his age. Good on him.

Likewise Bruce Forsyth (born 1928) who, in his eighties, found a new generation of fans by hosting Have I Got News For You.

Just when you thought he'd be spending more time with his golf clubs. All together now: good gameshow, good gameshow!

Politics

Politics, which someone once described as 'showbiz for ugly people', has always had its fair share of wrinklies. Winston Churchill was 65 when he took over as war leader in 1940 and Menzies 'Ming' Campbell was around the same age when he took over the leadership of the Lib Dems in 2006.

Some members of the House of Lords are believed to be some of the oldest people ever to have lived, putting their remarkable longevity down to lots of champagne, foie gras, and plenty of sleep (on those nice comfy red benches).

Sport

True, there aren't many wrinklies in the England football squad, so caps off to Brazilian professional Pedro Ribeiro Lima who scored his first goal at the age of 58 for his club Perilima in 2007.

Tennis player Martina Navratilova won the US Open mixed doubles in 2006 just before her 50th birthday and she won the Ladies Invitation Doubles trophy with Jana Novotna (41) at Wimbledon in 2010.

George 'The Fossil' Blanda played professional American football until the grand old age of 49 in 1976. Somehow it's quite comforting to know that someone else was being called a fossil at that relatively young age.

And if you play golf you won't be considered a fossil for quite some time. The oldest person to play in the PGA championships was Jerry Barber who was just a couple of months short of his 78th birthday at the time.

Tough stuff

It's usually younger people who climb mountains, but who takes them up? That's right, bony old grey-haired Sherpas.

In 2004 George Burnstad (what is it with these Georges?) swam the channel at the age of 70.

There simply isn't room to list all wrinkly achievements, but rest assured, they've done the lot. Whether it was John Glenn going up in the space shuttle Discovery at the age of 70 or Kirk Douglas becoming a blogger at 92 or Methuselah simply making it to the age of 969, it's pretty impressive. A wrinkly thumbs up to all concerned!

The Seven Habits Of Highly Effective Wrinklies

You may have read those motivational books about how highly successful people live their lives, and the things they all have in common that have made them the successes they are. Hell, you may even be one of those highly successful people! What they don't tell you though is how to be a highly effective wrinkly.

This is a separate skill in its own right, and here for the first time anywhere, are the secrets that you must be aware of to be a highly successful wrinkly.

1) Embrace wrinklyhood. There's no point in going into denial. Say it loud, you're wrinkly and you're proud!

2) Try something new. There's nothing worse than being a wrinkly in a wrut, sorry, rut. Go clubbing, show those youngsters a thing or three!

3) Learn a martial art. Muggers see wrinklies as an easy target. Thanks to CCTV your heroics may even end up on YouTube.

4) Buy a walk-in bath before you actually need one, then it'll look like you don't really need one when you do need one (if you see what we mean).

5) Sell your house now and live in luxury in a rented room – why leave it to those ungrateful relatives/government?

6) You know how there's always someone worse off than you? Well there's always someone older too. Be their young friend!

7) Compared with the future you, you're relatively young – hold on to that thought!

The Official Wrinkly-Way Code (aka The Wrinklies' Guide To The Road)

Wrinklies are to the road as confused tourists are to the Angel of the North – slightly bewildered, a bit dumbstruck, and wondering where the nearest toilet is.

We don't really do roads very well do we? Everyone whizzing around far too fast, too much noise and pollution and confusion reigning all around us.

For many wrinklies the road from A to B is more likely to feel like it could be the road from A to A&E. The quicker we're back in our comfy houses the better. Which is why we sometimes cut corners, ignore a few of the niceties of road usage and try to get the hell out of there. Who can blame us? It's dangerous out there.

So, here are a few Wrinkly rules of the road:

- All road users under the age of 50 are idiots – treat with extreme caution.
- When crossing the road the little green man always starts flashing when you're halfway across, so ignore him and step out whenever you feel like it.
- Road signs showing old people are ageist and should be pulled down or blown up by all self-respecting wrinklies.
- Speed limits are only guidelines so if you feel safer going at 15mph then ignore all those idiots behind you tooting their horns – even if you are in the fast lane of a motorway at the time.

- Motorised scooters are not cars so none of the rules of the road applies to them. Have fun!
- Road signs are all very well if you've got 20/20 vision, but unless they start printing the letters a bit bigger how the dickens are you supposed to follow them?
- Same with sat nav. However many times you say 'speak up a bit dear', she just carries on regardless. No wonder we get lost.
- Going slow is fine. Remember: overtakers end up at the undertakers.
- Remember the wrinklies' green cross code: stop, look, turn up your hearing aid.
- If you get too close behind a large vehicle he can't see you in his rear-view mirror, so that's the perfect time to give him a V sign for getting in your way.
- If you get stopped by a policeman asking for your licence, first feign deafness, then spend ten minutes rooting round in the glove box for your reading glasses, before beginning the search for your licence. Eventually he'll get fed up and leave you alone.
- When walking, always take a stick, then when you want to cross a busy road simply hold up your stick and dodder about on the kerb till someone stops. Why faff around looking for proper crossings?
- The Highway Code says the correct stopping distance when travelling at 30mph is 23 metres. However, as most wrinklies don't think in metres, let's call it about the length of the downstairs hall and halfway down the kitchen.

Songs For Wrinklies To Sing To Grandchildren At Bedtime

'The Wheels On My Chair Go Round and Round'

'Wee Willy Wrinkly'

'Necks, Shoulders, Knees and Toes (and Other Rheumatic Places)'

'Pop! Goes My Back Again'

'Zippered His Doo-dah (Poor Old Grandad)'

'If you're Happy and You Know It, You're Not a Wrinkly'

'There's a Hole In My Pension'

'Bah, Bah Humbug, Christmas Costs Too Much'

'One, Two Buckle My Shoe please, I can't Reach That Far Anymore'

'Skip To The Loo'

'There Was An Old Lady Who Swallowed a Fly (That'll Teach Her to Fall Asleep When She's Out For a Drive)'

'This Little Wrinkly Went to the Hypermarket (Where the gin's only a fiver a bottle)'

'Incy Wincy Pension'

'Wrinkly Had a Little Lamb (Have you seen the price of it these days?)'

Wrinklies With Attitude

When you reach wrinklyhood - and it comes to us all
– you may get a bit of flak. Particularly from younger
members of your family and friends. Jokes about bus
passes, forgetting things, walking sticks... All good
knockabout stuff.

But you also get a bit of aggro from shop assistants, bus
drivers, checkout staff and so on.

They seem to think that grey hair on your head equals
no grey matter inside it.

They seem to think that your inability to immediately
find your loyalty card on demand at the checkout is due to
the fact that your age is the equivalent of quite a good golf
score.

Patronising gits!

Even politeness grates. Do you want my seat on the
bus? What, because I wear bifocals? Do I want help
crossing the road? Listen, Sunny Jim, I've been crossing the
road by myself since you were in nappies. What do you
mean, 'exactly, grandad'?

Ooh, it makes your blood boil doesn't it? And no jokes
about blood pressure, if you don't mind.

The fact is, that when you become a wrinkly (and
when exactly is that, by the way? Are you totty one day,
and tottery the next?) you have to build up some defence
mechanisms, a bit of a tough skin.

In other words: a wrinkly with attitude. And here
are a few examples of how to handle yourself in certain
situations:

On the buses

When you try to swipe your library card instead of your freedom pass and the driver tuts while you look for your reading glasses just remind him how lucky he is that you're not still driving – then he'd really have something to complain about.

In the shops

When the checkout person asks 'do you want any help packing?', just say, 'I can pack my own groceries thank you very much, and I can pack a punch as well if necessary'. It usually works.

In the pub

When the barman makes a sarcastic comment about you making half a pint of bitter last three hours politely remind him that it takes roughly three hours to 'earn' enough state pension to pay for his overpriced beer in the first place.

At home

When someone comments about how unsocial it is for you to nod off during family gatherings ask them if it's any more social to be texting, listening to iPods, playing computer games or playing virtual tennis on an electronic gadget that sounds like a slightly unpleasant bodily function.

Kids

When kids ask you about the war, gently tell them you can just about remember the Falklands, and possibly Vietnam, and no, you have no direct experience of dinosaurs either.

Wrinklies Through History

As you lie down in your bed for the night, why not consider the achievements of the wrinkly ancestors who have gone before you!

The Missing Wrink

It has often been wondered how, in evolutionary terms, a happy-go-lucky 30-something can suddenly turn into a wrinkly. Scientists and anthropologists believe they have now found the answer. A skeleton has been found in the chalk hills of Dorset which appears to be the missing link between the two sub-species. The Missing Wrink, as he has been dubbed, has one over-developed hand, a result of writing letters of complaint to various tabloid newspapers and commercial organisations, one deaf ear that can be turned towards those he does not wish to listen to, and a comfy cardigan.

The Cave-Dwelling Wrinkly

He hunted for bargains with his club card and he invented the wheel... Well, the wheelchair. He was also the first person in human history not only to discover fire but also to complain about a winter fuel payment from the government to help keep it going during the cold months.

Wromulus and Wrinkmus

According to legend, the twins who originally founded the city of Rome. Wromulus was however left to do most of the heavy lifting involved in establishing the city because his ageing brother Wrinkmus was suffering from a bit of gyp in his back at the time.

Wrinklius Caesar

Under his rule, the Roman Empire fell. The Roman Empire then had to phone a special emergency number and wait until someone came to help get it back up again.

Attila the Wrinkly

Rampaged across Europe in the fifth century AD causing death, destruction, and rather a lot of complaints about people parking outside his house. He famously went up and across the Alps sitting on the back of an elephant or, as he described it, on an early design of stairlift.

Wrinkly the Conquerer

William's lesser-known brother who got lost on the way to Hastings and ended up a bit further over to the west. Here his wrinkly invasion force took over several south coast seaside resorts and made damn sure there were plenty of nice tea rooms, conveniently placed benches and disabled parking bays.

Wrinkhard The Lionheart

Early recipient of transplant surgery.

King Wrinkly VIII

Had six wives whom he treated appallingly badly. None bore him a son and heir so he bored them to death with tales of his wartime exploits, his love of single gauge steam railway trains and a non-stop diatribe against the failings of the local council's rubbish collection 'service'.

William Wrinkspeare

Very nearly the most famous writer in the English language. Unfortunately he never got round to composing a single play or line of poetry because he spent his entire career composing letters of complaint to the local paper.

Napoleon Wrinklyparte

A man who moaned so much about the way things were being run by the local council that he somehow ended up as Emperor with much of Europe under his command. He then attempted to invade Russia but gave up when he found there was no disabled access to the country. He was ultimately defeated at Waterloo, the name of which put him at a severe disadvantage. At the height of battle he kept feeling like he needed to find the nearest gents. He spent the last few years of his life stuck on the remote South Atlantic island of Saint Helena. Historians now believe this was as a result of buying an ill-advised timeshare property.

Ludwig Van Wrinkhoven

Wrote nine symphonies and every movement of every single one of them is slow. When people suggested that his music would be more popular if he occasionally speeded it up a bit, he always gave the same response: 'Pardon?'

Albert Wrinklestein

Formulated the Theory of Relatives: the more they visit, the more they are hoping to be left lots of money in your will.

Gypsy Rose Wrinklee

Ageing striptease artist and burlesque dancer who appalled audiences worldwide with her act which left nothing to the imagination, though many wished it had. 'Get 'em off!' her audience would cry at the start of her act before changing their tune abruptly a few seconds later and yelling in horror, 'Put 'em back on again!'

Wrinkly Churchill

No relation to our great wartime leader of course, but a stout defender of the rights of wrinklies everywhere with his stirring speeches such as 'We shall fight on the beaches, on the landing, down in the front room, in the fields and on the streets, and if the buggers try to put us into old people's homes we shall never surrender.'

Tim Berners-Wrinklee

Invented Ye Olde Worlde Wide Web to keep wrinklies in touch with one another worldwide. Some of the innovations wrinklies have him to thank for include: Social nitpicking sites, online carbon-dating (to determine the real ages of prospective computer dates), and an online marketplace for selling and swapping ill-fitting false teeth – ebaygum. He invented several other things as well but unfortunately although he had invented them they turned out to be a bit too complicated for him to be able to get them to work, and so they were lost to the world.

Chapter 3: Things That Go Wrinkly In The Night

Are you suffering from things going wrinkly in the night? Your curtains, sheets, pyjamas or nightie? Or is it the contents of your pyjamas or nightie that are revealed in the light of dawn as slightly more wrinkly than you remembered them looking yesterday?

How can this be?

We are regularly advised that in order to keep looking young and beautiful, we should try and get as much sleep as possible. But, like all advice that we are ever given by other people, this is clearly complete rubbish!

Young people never sleep. They're up every night drinking, taking drugs, having sex, dancing until dawn and chronicling the whole hideous experience on Facebook. And yet despite their complete lack of sleep, young people still look young.

We wrinklies however usually spend most of the day looking forward to toddling off to bed the moment that the clock strikes ten in the evening. Often we look forward to this highlight of the day from the moment we get out of bed in the morning. And yet despite spending our entire lives either asleep or looking forward to getting back to sleep, we still look old.

If only nature was a bit fairer. If only we really did look and feel younger as a direct result of the total amount of sleep we had had during our lives.

That way the older you became the more young and beautiful you would begin to look.

As a result of the cumulative amount of sleep experienced over a lifetime, a 60-year-old would end up looking youthful and gorgeous. Twenty-year-olds on the other hand who had not yet lived long enough to experience sufficient amounts of beauty enhancing sleep would look haggard and dreadful.

Old people would look young while young people would look old!

Surely that's got to be a fairer system!

Of course there is an obvious reason why older people are wrinklier than the young. The old have all clearly made the mistake of having once been young.

The wrinkles and jutting mounds of sagging flesh that have come to the surface in later life are in fact the remnants and reminders of parties and drinking sessions from years before.

The young may chronicle all their exciting experiences on Facebook but really there's no need. In a few years they'll have an abundance of unsightly protuberances and lines etched into their ageing flesh to remind them instead.

Each sign of age is a little message posted from the past!

The dark lines under your eyes are like a Twitter message from your younger self telling you what a great time they were having at an all night rave. The lines on your face are like a text you posted a few decades earlier to tell your ageing self what fun you were having at a 24-hour orgy.

OK, in retrospect it might have been better if you'd just kept a diary instead!

Wrinklies' Bedtime Routine

To keep healthy it is important for us wrinklies to follow a very strict bedtime routine every night (n.b. when we say strict, we don't mean getting someone dressed as an old fashioned school teacher to bend you over the bedstead and cane you within an inch of your life).

Nevertheless following a regular routine as you prepare yourself for bed will help you relax, unwind and enjoy the full eight, nine, ten or twenty three-and-a-half hours sleep your body now requires each night.

Firstly remember that eating late in the evening will give your stomach insufficient time to digest your food. Disturbed slumber will then result either from indigestion, burping in your sleep or the duvet being repeatedly blown off by the noxious guffs exuding from the bottom of your pyjamas.

Instead it is recommended that you eat your main meal as early as possible in the evening – preferably the night before. You should also avoid late night barbecues – particularly after you've got into bed.

Next avoid any activities during the evening that are likely to over exert your system and cause your heart rate to dramatically increase. For most people these side effects might result from participation in extreme sports, rampant sex and/or drug taking.

We wrinklies however are able to save time, effort and money because we are able to dramatically increase our heart rates just by walking up the stairs a bit too quickly.

Of course it can be difficult to avoid going up the stairs at bedtime (unless you live in a bungalow or have really given up on life). This is why wrinklies often end up having a stairlift installed in their homes. Thanks to stairlift technology, wrinklies can get up the stairs to bed without setting their pulses racing so fast that they are left unable to sleep for the rest of the night.

Don't forget also that a closed door will prevent a fire from spreading during the night. So if you find a fire blazing in your living room just before you go to bed, pick it up using a large shovel and put it in the cupboard under the stairs until morning when you can take it out and put it back in the living room again. So in conclusion:

- You must go to bed at exactly the same time every single night.
- You must follow the same strict routine as you prepare to sleep.
- You must secure your home against night-time intruders, burglars, murderers, arsonists and hoodlums.
- You must prepare for bed in exactly the same way every single night.
- You must then lie in bed in the same position as the night before whether you really want to or not while putting all thoughts of intruders, burglars, murderers, arsonists and hoodlums out of your mind.

Once you have done all these things it will be possible for you to finally relax and enjoy a good night's sleep!

Wrinkly Thoughts About Health, Diet And Exercise

- Being healthy is of course the slowest rate at which it is possible to die. And if you eat and drink sensibly as well, this will make the time pass even more slowly.

- Stay healthy as you get older but try not to look too good because otherwise younger people will never do anything to help you.

- If you manage to maintain a perfect physique into later life, after a certain age others will no longer regard you as being healthy but a freak!

- When people tell you 'you're extraordinary for your age', this is usually only a good thing if you are under 20 or over 70 years old.

- You wouldn't think that a small piece of cake could possibly hurt you – the name 'Death By Chocolate Cake' is a bit of a hint though.

- Don't forget that no pain equals no gain. So that's a handy way to remember how to avoid pain.

- Healthy versus wealthy: if you are healthy it doesn't matter if you aren't wealthy (because if you're healthy you can rob other people and run away in time).

- You can always say that you are allergic to health food.

- Chew each mouthful at least 20 times. After one mushroom you'll be exhausted.

- Look on the bright side! As long as you've got your health, you should have no trouble getting to the off licence and back.

The Wrinkly Guide To Staying Healthy

Get plenty of exercise:

One way for a wrinkly to do this is to spend years eating as much as possible thus becoming grossly overweight. The overweight wrinkly will then have to expend considerable effort and thus get plenty of exercise just by lugging his or her own enormous body around the place!

Take up jogging:

It would be unwise for a wrinkly to try jogging too far at first. Start off with quite short distances, for example to the biscuit tin and back. Remember, if you try jogging to the kettle and back you will probably spill your cup of tea on the return journey.

Eat your five-a-day:

There are lots of ways for wrinklies to get their five portions of fruit and veg a day: Jaffa Cakes, tomato sauce, cheese and onion crisps, strawberry jelly or, to get all five daily portions of fruit in one handy pack, a packet of Fruit Pastilles! But yes – that does mean you're not allowed to leave the green ones!

Give up drinking and smoking:

Of course if you don't drink and smoke to begin with this will mean you have to start by taking them both up.

Get one of those computer game/workout things:

With a Wii console or similar, it is possible for the average wrinkly to work up a considerable sweat. And that's just from trying to wire the thing up and getting it to work.

What Your Night Drink Says About You

Hot chocolate	Choco-holic
Glass of scotch	Alcoholic
Cup of tea	Tea-aholic
Horlicks	Horlic-aholic
Ovaltine	You are likely to burst into the Ovaltiney song at any moment. 'We are the Ovaltineys, Little girls and boys...' See! You've started already!
Hot milk	You've forgotten to buy any cocoa powder, haven't you?
Hot water	Not only did you forget the cocoa powder, you forgot the milk and sugar as well – or did you get a bit mixed up and pour a mug full of hot chocolate into your hot water bottle by mistake?
Cold water	Bloody hell! The electricity's gone off now!
Triple espresso	If you can get to sleep after drinking this, you really must be knackered
Several large scotches	You have such an excess of energy, you need to be completely sedated last thing every night in order to stop you careering around the place. So it's either this or your spouse has to shoot you with a tranquiliser dart
Can of energy drink	Unless you consume 800x your daily recommended allowance of caffeine, you can't muster the energy to get up the stairs to bed

The Wrinkly's Guide To Fad Diets

The F Plan Diet:

You eat a bit of roughage with everything. So it's obvious what the 'f' stands for - the Fart Yourself Thinner Diet!

The Raw Food Diet:

You can eat whatever you like as long as it's raw! This will definitely help you lose weight. Eating a single raw potato for example will take up much of the day while requiring a considerable amount of energy in the process. You will therefore not only lose weight but gain a highly developed jaw muscle. You can then move on to try and eat a raw cow.

The Cabbage Diet

You eat absolutely nothing except cabbage. Not only will you lose weight, you will also lose the will to live.

The Grapefruit Diet:

You eat endless amounts of grapefruit. This helps you lose weight because you are constantly being blinded by the grapefruit juice squirting up into your face when you plunge your spoon in. As a result of this temporary loss of sight you will be incapable of finding the biscuit or cake tins.

The Atkins Diet

You are only allowed to eat people with the surname Atkins. Also known as the Cannibal Conviction Solitary Confinement Prison Diet.

Ways To Avoid Going Quite So Wrinkly In The Night

A guide to natural remedies that can be applied over night to help reduce fine lines (or alternatively to fill in great canyon-like wrinkles like yours).

Cucumber over the eyes

These are traditionally used to hydrate the area around the eyes and to prevent dark oily patches forming. Another way to stop dark oily patches forming is to avoid spending each night lying in your driveway beneath the back axle of your car.

If you choose to place cucumbers over your eyes, remember to use sliced cucumbers. Don't lie there with two full grown vegetables on your face. If you do it will be extremely difficult to lie still for the entire night balancing a cucumber sticking up from each eye socket.

The danger will also exist that if you sit up suddenly during the night, you may catch a cucumber on your bedstead and put your eye out. This would prove that cucumbers aren't so good for your eyes after all.

Also the sight of you lying with two full grown cucumbers sticking up from your eyes may give your spouse a nasty turn if they wake up during the night. Seeing you in the half light, your spouse will be sure to assume that some horned figure from hell is occupying the other side of the bed rather than you squinting like mad to hold a pair of 12 inch cucumbers in your eye sockets.

So instead carefully place a slice of cucumber over each eye. Dangers may still exist however. In particular you may wake up, open your eyes, see nothing but a pair of enormous cucumbers and shriek in terror believing that you have fallen into a enormous vat of salad during the night.

Once morning comes don't forget to remove the cucumbers before you get up or they will be perceived by others as a new pair of humorous novelty spectacles and by yourself as an alarmingly sudden development of light green cataracts.

Tea bags over the eyes

You can try putting tea bags over your eyes instead of cucumbers. This may however cause a slight burning sensation particularly when you pour some hot water from the kettle over them to brew up.

Carrots up the nose

This ploy, similar to that of cucumbers over the eyes, is used by wrinklies who wish to avoid bags and oily circles forming under their nostrils.

Be careful however. If you sneeze during the night a carrot may be fired from one or other of your nostrils and spear your cat like an enormous orange dart.

Elastic bands

Wrinkles form as the result of a loss of elasticity. Sadly nature does not provide replacement elasticity. However your local stationery shop does! Why not try stretching a few elastic bands round your face to pull out the wrinkles over night? Or, alternatively, large strategically placed paper clips may do the trick.

Egg yolk over the skin

Rubbing egg yolk, lemon juice and olive oil into your face may help reduce dry rough skin.

Plus if you go to sleep with this mixture splattered over yourself and wake up with the sun shining directly onto your bed in the morning, you may find a sizzling pancake cooking on your face ready for your breakfast.

Pineapples on the wrinkles

Applying slices of pineapple to your face will help reduce visible wrinkles. It is however quite difficult to keep it balanced there and when you walk down the street you may attract comments along the lines of: 'Why is that wrinkly old person wandering around with bits of pineapple stuck all over their mush?'

For really deep wrinkles, hollow out an entire pineapple. Then stick your head inside it. Remember to make a couple of eye holes first.

Lemon juice in the wrinkles

Rubbing squeezed lemon juice into your wrinkles may make them magically disappear over night. Or alternatively it might make them extremely sore. Then when you wake up the next morning your wrinkles will not only still be there but they will be standing out better than ever because they are glowing bright red!

And if you do fill any particularly deep wrinkles with lemon juice don't forget there is then the possibility that next time you grin or grimace, this will cause citric acid to squirt sideways from your face thereby blinding those standing around you.

Yoghurt

Plain yoghurt smeared over the face is used in many exotic beauty regimes. Just slap a large tub of yoghurt all over your wrinkly chops until you look as though a passing emu has shed its load on you during the night.

If you don't have a plain yoghurt then why not use something else from the fridge? A 'fruit corner' yoghurt for example has the advantage that you can put the yoghurt over your cheeks and the fruit over your eyes.

This mix should then be left overnight after which skinflint wrinklies can try and scoop it back into the plastic pot again ready for that night's dinner.

Eating the mixture after it has been sitting on your face for an entire night is obviously rather disgusting and unhygienic. So try to fix it so your spouse ends up getting it for their pudding instead of you.

Two beef burgers, a portion of chips and a couple of doughnuts on the face

Not so much a beauty treatment as a late night snack. The food is laid out on the face (in the absence of a plate) making it both easier to locate in the darkness and easier to consume without having to completely wake up.

This treatment may help the skin on your face to tingle and glow but this will only occur if the food is applied to the cheeks straight from a hot frying pan.

Chapter 4:
A Book At Bedtime

In theory we wrinklies can read a book at any time, especially if we're retired wrinklies, but the bedtime book is something else entirely. It's a sleeping tablet in book form. Just read a few pages and zzzzz – you're fast asleep.

This probably means that to be truly effective as an aid to sleep your bedtime reading matter should be as boring as possible. *The Political Diaries of Geoffrey Howe* perhaps, cooking for vegans with nut allergies maybe, the history of cross-stitch...

But sometimes you don't want to nod off after just a couple of pages, especially if you've gone to bed at a wrinkly-friendly 9.30 pm.

You want to plump up your pillows, get the hot water bottle into exactly the right position to warm your wrinkled toes, have your bedtime drink placed within the required optimum range of your outstretched arm and get a couple of chapters under your pyjama rope belt before you enter the land of nod.

On the other hand you don't want to be over-stimulated by hair-bristling horror stories, steamy sex novels or by the spine-tingling and frankly shocking fine print of your pension plan.

Like most things in life, it's a fine balance.

Yes, the wrinkly book at bedtime is ideally the literary equivalent of a mild curry. Something that will tickle the taste buds rather than throttle them to death and something that will satisfy the appetite without laying on the stomach like a house-trained brontosaurus and leave one wanting more, but not just yet, thank you very much.

In fact, there may be publishers out there who could see this as a possible gap in the market. Like everything else these days, books are all too often aimed at youngsters – i.e. people under 50.

Bookshops always seem to be selling biographies of young slips of things who've been on some dreadful reality TV show and then feel compelled to write their 'entire' life story at the age of 19, or chick lit or lad lit or some other daft thing aimed at people who probably can't even read anyway.

No, what we need is old git lit. We don't want to read about 20-somethings called Lucy and Katy and Jake and Tarquin who all work in advertising agencies and drink skinny lattes all day. We want to read about people of our own age, people who've lived a bit, possibly who've died a bit too, people whose idea of a bit of excitement is finding a new crisp flavour at the supermarket.

We don't want doorstop blockbusters about crazed serial killers, we want nice autobiographies by celebrity gardeners. We don't want sex and shopping novels, just the shopping is fine, if it's all the same to you.

There's a whole, vast, untapped market out there for some enterprising publisher. Imagine the titles: *The Girl With the Dralon Tattoo*, *The Bus Traveller's Daughter*, *Captain Corelli's Ear Trumpet*...

Goodnight wrinklies everywhere! (Hope that exclamation mark didn't wake you up).

Rip Van Wrinkly And Other Role Models

Rip Van Wrinkly

The world of fiction is full of role models for wrinklies. Take Rip Van Wrinkly for example, Rip Van Winkle's lesser-known brother. He slept for a hundred years, then woke up and sued the local health authority who prescribed his super strength sleeping tablets. That'll teach 'em.

Chubb-locked Homes

The brilliant detective who never had a single case to solve because he joined his Neighbourhood Watch team and encouraged everyone in the locality to have locks on every door, window, skylight and catflap to keep the thieving beggars out.

Pilly Bunter

What's the use of free medical care if you don't use it? You've paid in all your life, so now it's time to take something out. You can get pills to help you sleep, pills to wake you up, pills to help you eat, pills to keep off the weight, pills to make you go to the loo... well, you get the picture.

Long Johns Silver

At a certain time in our life we don't want to be wearing skimpy underwear. Too skimpy, and it might even get lost under the rolls of fat and defeat the object of wearing any at all. No, on reaching wrinkliehood the only option is several yards of cotton that will cover everything, dangling or otherwise. And if you happen to be a limb-deficient pirate, the all-covering underwear will also disguise the fact that you have a wooden leg.

Harry Chamberpotter

Who wants to go stumbling around in the dark at the dead of night? You wake up at three o'clock sweating from a terrible dream about being stuck in a lift with an earnest young politician and you have an uncontrollable desire to rush to the toilet. Rushing, these days, is not in your repertoire so a quick feel under the bed and out comes the old faithful 'gazunder'. Perfect.

Robinson Creosote

Not for him the idling around at weekends so beloved by the younger generation. No, there are a thousand and one little jobs around the house that can be found if you put your mind to it. And if you ever think you've run out of little jobs you can always creosote the fence, or the shed, or anything else in the garden made of wood. The Devil makes work for idle hands and all that. This person is not to be confused with Robinson Crusoe who got somebody else to do all his little jobs for him.

Peter Pan-acea

Aches and pains to the wrinkly are what cats and dogs are to the vet – they come with the territory. The big mistake most wrinklies make is to start to enlarge their medical cabinet to a size that Damien Hirst might consider to be a suitable installation for the Tate Modern's Turbine Hall. No! Far better to take a panacea, such as a nice box of chocolates, a drink or two, or even a crafty fag.

The Da Wrinkly Code

The Da Wrinkly Code is a little-known series of clues woven through literature to let wrinklies know the meaning of life.

In 2004 an author by the name of Dan Brown published a book entitled *The Da Vinci Code* which has no connection whatsoever with the Da Wrinkly Code.

One of the classic books to contain clues for the Da Wrinkly Code is *Alice in Wonderland*. Many wrinklies have a bottle of sherry on the sideboard which has the invisible words 'drink me' written on it.

When a wrinkly gives up work (or vice versa) and has a bit more time on his or her hands, the words 'drink me' seem to take on an almost supernatural luminosity.

Whereas at one time the cork would not be popped until the sun was over the yard arm, or at least until the six o'clock news had started, in the timeless half-life of retirement one hour merges into another so that before you know where you are you're having a quiet tipple with your cornflakes.

Alice in Wonderland also contains a metaphor for ageing: that of the shrinking person. As the years roll by wrinklies find that not only are policemen getting younger, they're getting taller as well! This can be simultaneously comforting and rather disconcerting.

In Charles Dickens' *A Christmas Carol* the wrinkly will find the ultimate role model in Ebeneezer Scrooge. Not for him the shallow pursuit of pleasure, the sunny nature, the modern obsession with dishing out money to layabouts, ne'er-do-wells, and charities for people who should lift themselves up by their own bootstraps instead of sponging off others. He has the old fashioned virtues of thrift, hard work and clipping kids round the ear if they get out of hand.

But some clues in the Da Wrinkly Code are harder to spot than others. Have you ever been on a stairlift? Close your eyes and you may experience a sensation similar to that of flying. Just like Peter Pan!

Neverland is of course retirement, Captain Hook is the Chancellor of the Exchequer, wickedly keeping your pension low, Tinkerbell is the personification of wrinkly charities such as Help The Aged, and the Lost Boys are those wrinklies who end up on park benches drinking strong cider out of cans. It all makes perfect sense now doesn't it?

Look through your bookshelves and find your own clues in the Da Wrinkly Code. Once you start you'll be amazed at how many there are.

1984: Winston Smith battling against an overweening state which has CCTV cameras everywhere and ministries that do the opposite of what they're supposed to; *Brave New World* where everyone's obsessed by sex and you're over the hill at 60; Kafka's *Metamorphosis* where you wake up and find you've turned into a giant insect – yet another wrinkly metaphor!

Yes, once you start to look, you'll find clues in the Da Wrinkly Code everywhere from Noddy to Godot.

Books To Read At Bedtime

Don Quixote – Miguel de Cervantes

An inspirational book for wrinklies everywhere. Retired 50-something wrinkly decides life is a bit dull and goes off in search of adventure. Sensibly, Don Quixote doesn't go off to fight dragons or anything dangerous like that; he has a pop at something not likely to fight back – windmills.

Pride And Prejudice – Jane Austen

The marvellous thing about reading the classics is that you've seen so many films, TV adaptations, pop-up books and so on that you can skip the boring bits and still know what's going on. P&P also won't be so exciting that you can't nod off eventually.

Ulysses – James Joyce

A 'stream of consciousness' book that with a bit of luck will result in a stream of unconsciousness from you if you're finding it hard to get off to sleep. One sentence alone is over 4,000 words long, so who knows, you may not even get to the end of that before drifting away.

Dr Zhivago – Boris Pasternak

Simply imagine that he's your doctor, and you're running through your usual little list of ailments. You'll be sleeping like a baby in no time. It also has the advantage of not boring your usual doctor to death with all this stuff too.

The Picture of Dorian Gray – Oscar Wilde

The concept of a picture in your attic that ages while you stay eternally young should be of great appeal to wrinklies everywhere.

Books Not To Read At Bedtime

War of the Worlds – H.G. Wells

Surburbia should be a place of sanctuary for wrinklies. It's bad enough when you get hoodies invading your peace and quiet, but Martians in Woking? It's hardly conducive to a good night's kip is it?

Moby Dick – Herman Melville

After reading about someone being attacked by a whale it would be terrifying to find in the night that your amply-proportioned other half has rolled over you and made you feel as if you were reliving the fate of Captain Ahab.

Brighton Rock – Graham Greene

Although you may once have associated Brighton with Mods and Rockers having punch-ups on the beach, it may now well be the sort of place you'd go to for a nice day out. You may not sleep so easy in your bed though after reading about Graham Greene's low-life gangsters going round murdering people.

Les Miserables – Victor Hugo

Reading the book shouldn't be a problem, but if you've seen the musical and it keeps prompting you to break into song every few pages then you won't be popular with your spouse, your neighbours, or any music lovers who are within earshot.

The Gruffalo – Julia Donaldson & Axel Scheffler

How old are you exactly?

Opening Lines Of Novels That Wrinklies Can Identify With

A Tale of Two Cities – Charles Dickens

It was the best of times, it was the worst of times – my daughter-in-law baked us some lovely scones but I can't find me teeth.

Pride And Prejudice – Jane Austen

It is a truth universally acknowledged, that a single man in possession of a good fortune, must be in want of a wife and that if he finds one he won't be in possession of a good fortune for very much longer.

Lolita – Vladimir Nabakov

Lolita, light of my life, fire of my loins, get your clothes back on and pretend to carry on cleaning.

Mrs Dalloway – Virginia Woolf

Mrs. Dalloway said she would buy the flowers herself. Well, it's her funeral so let the silly old cow do what she wants.

1984 – George Orwell

It was a bright cold day in April, and the clocks were striking thirteen – so all in all a typical morning waiting for a train in our wonderful country!

A Portrait of the Artist as a Young Man – James Joyce

Once upon a time and a very good time it was there was a moocow coming down along the road and this moocow that was coming down along the road wasn't stopped outside Waitrose for five minutes before a traffic warden slapped a ticket on its backside.

Fahrenheit 451 – Ray Bradbury

It was a pleasure to burn down the town hall when they put my council tax up again.

Rebecca – Daphne Du Maurier

Last night I dreamt I went to Manderley again, but of course this morning it was just the bottle bank and the library as usual.

To Kill a Mockingbird – Harper lee

When he was nearly 13 my brother Jem got his army badly broken at the elbow. And even now, at the age of 65 he still says it was me who pushed him out of that tree.

The Old Man and the Sea – Ernest Hemingway

He was an old man who fished alone in a skiff in the Gulf Stream as it was actually cheaper than trying to buy fresh fish in his local supermarket.

Anna Karenina – Leo Tolstoy

Happy families are all alike – teach your grandchildren to play a decent game like Bridge or Gin Rummy.

I, Claudius – Robert Graves

I, Tiberius Claudius Drusus Nero Germanicus This-that-and-the-other (for I shall not trouble you yet with all my titles) do solemnly declare that I shall tell the truth, the whole truth and nothing but the truth regarding the non-payment of my council tax due to the inadequate provision of disabled parking bays in the borough...

The Hobbit – J.R.R. Tolkein

In a hole in the ground there lived a Hobbit. Probably had to sell his house in order to fund nursing care, I shouldn't wonder.

Bedtime Stories For Wrinklies To Tell Their Grandchildren

Goldilocks and the Three Wrinklies

Once upon a time three wrinklies lived in a little wrinkly house in the woods. Mummy wrinkly, Daddy wrinkly, and a wrinkly little baby.

One day, a young girl named Goldilocks was walking through the woods when she stopped at the house. She saw on the door a picture of a ferocious looking Alsatian dog with the words 'I live here' on it. She saw the Neighbourhood Watch sticker on the window and the sign reading 'all visitors must show their ID'. She then noticed the burglar alarm on the wall and the sign reading 'no hawkers, circulars or beggars'. She then noticed a wrinkly face peeking out from behind the net curtains and saying 'clear off!' Goldilocks took the hint and decided to go to the three bears' house instead.

Little Red Riding Hoodie

Little Red Riding Hoodie was bunking off school one day, and she decided to go and visit her grandmother to see if she could blag some money for cigarettes and lip gloss.

When she got to her grandmother's house the door was open. 'Typical!' she thought to herself, 'Someone's already turned the place over and nicked Gran's money so I'll have to go shoplifting instead.'

But out of curiosity she looked inside, and there was a little hunched up figure sitting in her grandmother's armchair. But there was something odd about her.

'Blimey, Gran!' exclaimed little Red Riding Hoodie. 'What's occurring with your eyes? They're like, ginormous! And look at your teef - they're well out of order!'

It was then that Little Red Riding Hoodie remembered her grandmother didn't have any teeth, and she whisked off the shawl from her head.

'April fool!' shouted Gran from behind her. The daft old cow had dressed the dog up in her clothes.

The Three Wrinkly Goats Gruff

Once upon a time there lived three wrinkly goats gruff. One day the three wrinkly goats wanted to cross the river to get to another field where the grass was greener. The only problem was that on the other side of the bridge lived a troll. That's right, it was a troll bridge.

'What if he eats us?' asked the smallest of the wrinkly goats. He won't eat you,' said the middle-sized wrinkly goat, 'you're too small.'

'He won't eat either of you,' said the biggest wrinkly goat gruff. 'It's me he'll eat because I've got most meat on me.'

So the little wrinkly billy goat gruff went across safely and the middle-sized one did too.

The big billy goat gruff hesitated as he saw the troll waiting on the other side of the bridge.

Then the troll shouted out, 'You're all right mate I wouldn't want to eat a wrinkly if you paid me, I'm off for a pizza.'

The Three Little Wrinkly Pigs

Once upon a time there were three wrinkly pigs who lived in houses that were too big for them after their piglets had grown up and left home. Also, they were finding the council tax a bit steep so they decided to sell up and move into something smaller and cheaper.

The first wrinkly pig made himself a house out of straw but a bad wolf easily broke in and ate him up.

The second wrinkly pig built himself a house out of old walking sticks, but the bad wolf easily broke into that too and ate him up.

The third wrinkly pig was a bit cleverer and built himself a house made of bricks. And sure enough, the bad wolf couldn't get in.

However, an even badder council tax official turned up at the door and told him he would have to pay even higher council tax than he had before.

The moral of this story is: if you think getting eaten by a wolf is bad, don't mess with the council.

Wrinkly Rapunzel

Once upon a time a beautiful young girl named Rapunzel was locked in a tower by a wicked witch.

For many years Rapunzel lived in the tower despairing of ever being freed. She got older and older and her long golden locks turned to grey and as even more years passed by she gave up hope of ever being released.

Then one day, a handsome young prince stopped at the tower and called out: 'Rapunzel, Rapunzel, let down your hair!'

So Rapunzel leaned out of the tower and threw down her hair.

The prince caught the wig in his hand, looked up at the bald Rapunzel and rode off never to be seen again.

And he, at least, lived happily ever after.

The Wrinkly's New Clothes

There once lived a very wrinkly old man and every time he went to the local swimming pool, people laughed at his wrinkly old body.

So he went to a special shop for wrinklies that provided lifelike body suits without a wrinkle in sight.

The old man put the suit on and looked proudly at himself in the mirror. Not a single wrinkle! He turned this way and that and from whatever angle he looked all he could see was lovely smooth skin.

Later that day he went to the swimming pool, donned his wrinkle-free body suit and dived confidently off the top board.

As he did so, a young child cried out, 'He hasn't got any clothes on!'

Yes, the silly old wrinkly had put on the body suit all right, but had forgotten his swimming trunks. His case comes up next week.

Chapter 5:
Wrinkly Bedside Bits & Bobs

We all know it is prudent to keep certain items on your bedside table. These may often include a lamp, an alarm clock and maybe even a book or magazine to read.

That's not enough for wrinklies though. Over the years, wrinklies have built up a much more detailed and extensive itinerary of items that are vital to have within arm's reach during the night.

A small bedside table will never be enough for the average wrinkly. They will instead require some form of significantly sized storage unit with drawers, cabinets, a broad worktop, several bookshelves, possibly a few secret compartments and a small medical centre. It would probably be possible to open some wrinklies' bedside cabinets as small department stores.

Wrinklies have an obvious requirement for various medical supplies at their bedside. When the drawer of the wrinkly's bedside cabinet opens, it does so with a maraca-like rattle as several hundred pill bottles shudder into view. The wrinkly's bedside table is nothing short of a small pine effect life-support system. The addition of a small compartment in which a midget pharmacist could sit would surely be a welcome addition.

There are then various over-the-counter lotions, potions and of course the in-bedside-cabinet chiropodist's department. Here the wrinkly will store a range of items to help trim, smooth and pick bits off themselves should the need to do this suddenly arise at any time during the hours of darkness.

There will also be a phone on one side or the other of the wrinkly bed. Possibly both. This would thereby make it theoretically possible for the wrinkly on one side of the bed to call up the wrinkly on the other side to tell them to stop hogging the duvet.

In-bed entertainment will be another feature. No, not that sort of in-bed entertainment! There will however be a radio and a CD player somewhere on this vast bedside cabinet.

There will also be a remote control handy for the enormous but slightly outdated television that was moved from the living room a year ago (in order to make way for an even larger model) and which is now precariously balanced on the dressing table opposite the end of the bed.

And let's not forget the teasmade. This incredible machine sits on the bedside table and can be programmed to sound an alarm to wake you up and then present you with a freshly brewed cup of tea. Wrinklies will probably also have various other foodstuffs readily to hand.

Wrinklies are clearly working towards a point where they will have everything necessary to sustain life at their bedside: food, drink, medical supplies, TV, radio, communication systems with the outside world! Why bother getting out of bed again?

If only the whole set up could be made mobile so wrinklies could tootle down to the shops while still lying in bed.

Or is that the reason the bed has casters?

Essential And Less Essential Items For The Wrinkly Bedside

Bedside Essentials	Bedside Less Than Essentials	Maybe A Bit Over The Top To Have At The Bedside
Teasmade	Cappuccino maker	Fully licensed bar
Radio	CD player	DJ turntables plus dance area with mirror ball
Nail clippers	Callus knife and other implements to remove hard skin	Full hospital operating theatre equipment
Telephone	Mobile telephone	Switchboard operating system
Pills and other drug items prescribed by the doctor	Non-prescription/ illegal drug items	Extensive chemistry set with test tubes, a Bunsen burner and a white-coated assistant
Dry skin cream	Creams for every conceivable skin condition	Enough lotions to preserve an Egyptian mummy
An emergency contact telephone number	Telephone number for an emergency chiropractor	Hotline to your local Member of Parliament
Television	Surround sound cinema system	A small group of repertory players
A half read library book	A pile of books and magazines	A small branch of W H Smiths
A packet of biscuits	Microwave oven	Barbecue

Everything You Ever Wanted To Know About Beds

In ancient times only the very rich could afford beds. The poor were therefore not only poor but permanently quite tired although they did have an excellent opportunity to rob from the rich while the rich were snoozing away on their expensive beds.

The first bed raised off the ground was introduced around 3,400 BC. Coincidentally it was around this time that DFS started their sale which, as we all know, is still going on to this day.

In *The Odyssey*, Odysseus's bed is described as being made of a woven rope. A rope would however be extremely difficult to balance on for an entire night particularly if you fell asleep at any stage.

An additional danger associated with the rope bed was that an intruder could pull on the ropes during the night and thus use them to catapult you out of your bedroom window.

Mattresses were originally stuffed with straw. The effect must therefore have been like trying to get to sleep balanced on a giant Weetabix.

The expression 'sleep tight' is said to come from tightening the ropes used to support mattresses during the 16th century. Or alternatively it means falling asleep because you're blind drunk.

Beds are still popular to this day. They are used by most people for sleeping and procreation purposes and by wrinklies as places beneath which they can keep lots of stuff they have bought but which they never seem to use.

Breakfast In Bed Wrinkly Style

Breakfast in bed is a much overrated luxury which inevitably results in spilt drinks and bits of food all over the sheets.

But then it is called breakfast in bed isn't it?

It also invariably leads to bouts of indigestion as a result of wrinklies attempting to eat and drink a large number of items in rapid succession whilst reclining in a semi-prone position without adequate back support.

The other reason breakfast in bed is a dubious pleasure is because it requires someone to get out of bed, go downstairs, prepare the sumptuous repast and carry it all back up the stairs balanced precariously on a small tray. They will then probably trip over the cat and unload the feast all over their partner who has remained snoozing in the bed.

Once again, it is literally breakfast in bed!

An amazing device was invented to save wrinkly marriages. This was the teasmade. This state of the art invention was designed to sit by the bedside and wake the wrinkly couple up each morning with a freshly made cup of tea. This would then be ruined by the addition of milk which had curdled after being left out by the bedside all night.

Ironically the teasmade in fact may have led to many divorces among wrinkly couples. Well, if you could get a machine to make you a cup of tea each morning very little reason seemed to remain for some wrinklies to stay with their partners.

Wrinklies Bedside Essentials: The Speaking Alarm Clock

Just what the sleepy wrinkly needs first thing in the morning. An alarm clock that wakes you up with an appropriately phrased message (spoken quite loudly in case you're a bit hard of hearing).

Choose from the following wrinkly wake up call messages:

- 'Come on! Get up! If you can hear this you are still alive... theoretically!'
- 'Attention! It is now time for you to wake up! This therefore means that everything that happens from this point on is no longer a dream but reality!'
- 'Wakey wakey, wrinkly wrinkly!'
- 'Get up, you lazy wrinkly! Hurry up and start moving or distant family members will begin staking their claims to your savings!'
- 'Get up! Shake a leg! Though at your age you better not shake it too vigorously!'
- 'It's a brand new day! There's a whole new world out there! It's time for you to get up and start moaning about things!'
- 'Good news and bad news for you this morning: the good news is that it is possible for you to smooth the wrinkles out of your bed sheets...'
- 'Wake up! Get out of bed as quickly as you can without risking giving yourself a heart attack!'

The Ultimate Wrinkly Bed

So what special features might the world's ultimate bed for wrinklies boast? How about:

Bizarrely misshapen mattress to exactly fit the contours of a wrinkly's bizarrely misshapen back.

Alarm built into bed covers which will sound if either of the wrinkly bed occupants tries to claim more than their fair share of the duvet.

Miniature beds along the bottom of the bed for the use of any wrinkly pets that share the bedroom.

Volume control knob on headboard to turn down the nocturnal noises produced by your wrinkly bed companion.

Gently vibrating mattress to send you to sleep at night before going into a more vigorous shaking cycle to wake you up in the morning.

Guttering round edge of bed to carry away any night-time dribble coming from sleeping wrinklies' mouths.

Thermostatic control attached to electric blanket to make sure wrinkly bed occupants' feet never drop below a certain temperature.

Microphone on bedstead attached to loud hailer on outside of house to directly address miscreant youths gathering in street outside, irritating neighbours arriving home late etc.

Small machine gun turret at end of bed in case of night-time intruders unexpectedly turning up in bedroom.

Bedtime Checklist

Going to bed as a wrinkly is not simply a case of walking
up the stairs, it's like the planning of a military campaign.
Dunkirk? Agincourt? Glastonbury? Mere child's play. A place
for everything and everything in its place. But you need never
be caught out again with this wrinkly bedtime checklist.

1) Bedtime drink. Whether it's malty and milky or malty
   and 70% proof just make sure it's nowhere the glass
   with your teeth in it – you could have a nasty shock.
2) Bedtime reading. Nothing too exciting now. You don't
   want your loins girded just before you try to get to
   sleep do you?
3) Cat out? There's nothing worse than being woken in
   the middle of the night by a great furry lump rubbing
   up against you and purring – and it's just as bad if it's
   the cat.
4) Doors and windows locked? The odds of getting
   murdered in your bed are probably about the same as
   Elvis crashing his UFO into your house, but best be
   on the safe side.
5) TV off? TV on standby uses as much electricity as
   cooking your morning toast. And if your other half
   finds you've been wasting electricity again you'll
   probably be toast.
6) Milk bottles out? You don't want to have to rush out
   at 5am in your dressing gown do you?
7) Torch handy for night-time loo excursions?

Goodnight wrinklies everywhere!

How To Adapt When Not Sleeping In Your Own Wrinkly Bed

Sleeping in a strange bed in a nice yet reasonably priced hotel can be a disarming experience for a wrinkly.

The following points should therefore be kept in mind:

Hotel beds may be loaded with six pillows or more. Do not attempt to spend the night with your head balanced precariously at the top of these unless you have a neck like a giraffe.

The bedding on hotel beds will be turned down ready for you in the evening in case you get confused about how to climb in. Your bed at home will be turned down ready for you because you didn't get around to making it that morning.

Hotel beds have crisp clean sheets. Maybe the reason you're so wrinkly is not because you're getting older but because you are covered in imprints from all the creases in your infrequently changed bedding at home.

Hotel beds may have a button at the side to press for room service. If you wish to have one of these installed at home, have it attached to a buzzer on the opposite side of your bed. You can then use it to wake your wrinkly partner to do your bidding!

Wrinklies should remember to remove the chocolate left on their hotel pillow before sleeping otherwise they will wake up with a large brown blob stuck firmly to the side of their heads and presume they have contracted some form of melanoma.

Wrinklies Bedside Essentials: The Teasmade-Cum-Defibrillator

A handy new invention for the wrinkly who might be having a bit too much of a lie in.

A nice cup of tea brewed by the teasmade machine at the side of the bed is usually enough to get anyone up and out of bed in the morning. Often this is because the tea made by the teasmade tastes so horrible they are forced to get up and go down to the kitchen to make themselves a proper drink instead.

However for those of us who sometimes need just a little more impetus to get up in the morning comes the teasmade cum defibrillator!

Yes, if the tea doesn't get you going, the hot plates from beneath the kettle and teapot double as defibrillator pads. Simply remove the tea crockery and put it in a safe place then pull out the defibrillator pads from the teasmade and attach them to the chest.

Then just flip the switch on the teasmade to the 'boil' setting and 1,000 volts will flow through the sleepy wrinkly's chest cavity. It should be just the jolt he/she needs to get out of bed in the morning!

And after this emergency cardiac arrest treatment, what could be nicer than to relax with a cup of tea heated up on the same electrically charged pads?

And remember this is the only defibrillator currently on the market to have a handy 'snooze' function setting!

Wrinkly Pyjamarama

If wrinklies had their own country, pyjamas and dressing gowns would be the national dress.

Pyjamas are loose, comfortable garments with elasticated waists thus making them ideal for wrinklies.

Pyjamas were first brought back to Europe from the Far East by the explorer Vasco Pyjama, a manager at a branch of Marks and Spencer, who had been out there for a sleepover.

When pyjamas were first introduced in the 18th century, people wore them at all times of the day. This tradition is maintained to this day by wrinklies.

Pyjamas are nowadays usually worn for sleeping. Wrinklies wear them during the day because they may fall asleep at any time.

A dressing gown is so called because if you are wearing one it means you don't have to bother dressing.

A smoking jacket is similar to a dressing gown, the only difference being that the smoking jacket has recently been ironed using too high a setting.

Children's pyjamas are often emblazoned with the image of a well loved cartoon character such as Winnie the Pooh or Spiderman. Popular designs for wrinklies' pyjamas include ones printed with pictures of Dame Vera Lynn, Winston Churchill, Mrs Thatcher and the man who invented Viagra.

Other popular patterns for wrinkly pyjamas include tartan, stripes, polka dots and varicose veins.

Pyjamas are usually highly unfashionable in design. They therefore will not clash with other items in the typical wrinkly's wardrobe.

Pyjamas are often garishly coloured or patterned which makes them easier to find if their wearer's eyesight isn't what it used to be.

Pyjama trousers offer very little to get in your way if you need to get to the toilet quickly. Again this proves pyjamas must have been specifically designed with the wrinkly wearer in mind.

Pyjama jackets usually have a single breast pocket specially designed to hold your handkerchief, glasses and teeth safely during the night.

Other forms of nightwear are available with erotic elements of design such as the peek-a-boo nightie or various crotchless items of apparel. Pyjama manufacturers were quick to respond to this demand with the non-buttoning wide open pyjama trouser fly.

The open trouser fly on a pair of pyjamas trousers makes them terrifying to others. This helps ensure that when pyjamas are worn in public, few people will bother you. Once again this makes them particularly attractive to wrinklies.

If you go to the shops wearing your pyjamas you will often be brought home by the police. This can save you a fortune on bus or taxi fares as well as providing a nice young man to carry your heavy shopping for you.

Nightwear For Wrinklies:
Not Recommended

The following are probably inappropriate forms of
nightwear for a wrinkly:

- Peek-a-boo nightie (particularly for male wrinklies)
- Anything with the word 'crotchless' in its title
- Anything with the word 'micro' in its name
- The form of night apparel described as 'au naturel'
  is also not recommended for wrinklies (it's probably
  best for wrinklies to stick to 'au completely artificial'
  these days)
- Anything too silky (when the wrinkly climbs into bed
  they will fly straight out of the bottom of the duvet
  like a piece of soap)
- Anything labelled 'see through' (that's not because
  wrinklies don't have beautiful bodies – of course they
  do! It's just that because of the poor state of their
  eyesight, if a wrinkly lays an item of see through
  nightwear down anywhere, they will probably never
  be able to find it again)
- Anything made from rubber (squeaking and farting
  noises will probably keep a wrinkly awake all
  night. And that's before we even get onto the noises
  produced by their rubber pyjamas)
- Anything made from acrylic material particularly when
  combined with nylon sheets (it will be like a lightning
  storm in the bedroom every time the wrinkly climbs into
  bed – on the other hand the resulting electrical charge
  might unexpectedly re-invigorate the wrinkly making
  them feel suddenly younger and more energetic)

Nightwear For Wrinklies: Recommended

The following forms of night apparel will probably look a bit more appropriate on a wrinkly and prove less distracting during the wee small hours:

- Warm comfortable sensible flannelette pyjamas or nightdress of course!
- A long nightshirt and pointy nightcap or bonnet. This outfit should preferably be set off with a burning candle standing on a little candle holder held in one trembling hand. Basically if a wrinkly ends up looking like something straight out of a Dickens novel that's probably about right. This form of nightwear has the added advantage that if any youths or local miscreants come knocking at the door after nine o'clock in the evening, the wrinkly can pretend to be a ghost and frighten them away!
- Anything with a blue check pattern (to match the patterns of a wrinkly's varicose veins).
- Eye mask and ear plugs and anything else that might blot out the awfulness of the modern world. Don't forget though if nose plugs are inserted as well these may cause asphyxiation.
- A dressing gown so thick, soft and cuddly it is possible for a wrinkly to trip over and bounce down the stairs while wearing it and not injure themselves in any way.
- Pyjamas with stripes that make a wrinkly look like an inmate at a maximum security prison.

The Wrinklies Guide To Bedtime Snacks

Bedtime snack	Reasons it might be inadvisable
Cheese and biscuits	Cheese! Before bedtime! You might as well make it hallucinogenic drugs and biscuits!
Piece of toast	Eat this in bed and afterwards it will be like trying to get to sleep while lying on a gravel pathway
Beans	Remember to open all windows and extinguish any naked flames
Breakfast cereal with milk	If you want to leave a pebbledash effect over your bed covers that's your business
Chips	Don't forget to have a range of clothes ready for the morning that are all two sizes larger than the ones you were wearing today
Pancakes	Your digestive system will spend the night making noises not unlike the opening of a Jean Michel Jarre album
Takeaway	Are you worried you're going to starve to death during the night? By morning your indigestion will not only have burnt right through your oesophagus, it will have singed a hole in your mattress as well
Dried fruit	We suppose it will get you up and out of bed nice and quick in the morning. Alternatively the build up of gas during the night may be sufficient to propel you from the bed like a circus performer fired from a cannon

Wrinklies Bedside Essentials: Luminous Dentures

These days we all know the importance of being green and counting the pennies. Well, why not do both?! Yes, you can save the energy and cost of expensive night-lights by getting yourself a set of luminous dentures! New Dentaglo ™ dentures are at the biting edge of tooth technology. Simply pop them into a glass of water at bedtime and leave on your bedside table. Their eerie dentalescent glow will then light up your bedroom throughout the night providing sufficient illumination to get you to the toilet and back as many times as you need. And as we all know that can be quite a lot of times!

> 'When I wake in the night it's as though there's always someone there smiling at me in the darkness.' *Mr P, London*

> 'It's like having the reassuring presence of the massive teeth of a ghostly Bee Gee beaming at you from the side of your bed.' *Mrs B, Devizes*

> 'I bought a set of Dentaglo ™ luminous dentures and people soon began to notice the difference. Particularly when I smiled at them during a temporary power cut.' *Mr S, Portsmout*

And that's not all! Dentaglo ™ luminous dentures can also be used as a small portable torch available at any time of the day or night. Looking to see if your car keys have fallen under the sofa? Simple! Just get down on your hands and knees and grin into the darkness!

Chapter 6:
Night-Time Prayers
For Wrinklies

Bedtime is the time when you get down on your knees and say your prayers. Wrinklies should however be careful when attempting this acrobatic feat. Make sure your panic alarm is to hand. Otherwise you might get down on your knees and discover that you can't get back up again afterwards.

You would then be left in a praying position for the entire night and by morning would have achieved a state of utmost serenity. Or hypothermia as it's sometimes known.

At least you'd be in the right position to pray for someone to come and help you. Failing that shouting and swearing at the top of your voice until assistance arrives is probably more effective, although less serene. Shouting and swearing will however probably involve frequent references to the deity.

Even if you are able to spring nimbly in and out of a kneeling position, wrinkly prayers may not always be conducted in quiet contemplation.

The praying wrinkly may intend to look back and give thanks for the day just gone. Unfortunately the day just gone has probably contained its fair share of frustrations and irritations. Before you know it, the wrinkly's prayer of thanksgiving has become a series of muttered curses on those who have crossed him/her during the day.

Nevertheless wrinklies are often looked upon as religious and spiritual leaders. Jobs such as Archbishop of

Canterbury or Pope are seldom given to those in the first flush of youth.

After all who would want to see his holiness come out on the balcony in St Peter's Square dressed in a hoodie, with a piercing in his eyebrow, showing off his new tattoo and doing a double thumbs up to the crowd by way of a blessing?

No, religious leaders tend to be the wrinkliest of the wrinkly. The more wrinkles you have, the more likely you are to get the job!

This is why you are very unlikely to see the leader of the Greek Orthodox Church fronting an advertising campaign for Oil of Olay or the Chief Rabbi turning to camera and saying the words, 'Because you're worth it!'

But why are we wrinklies perceived as being so holy that it seems that any of us might be given a job as leader of one of the world's great religions apparently at random?

Perhaps people believe we have lived so long we have reached a deep understanding of life. They obviously fail to notice that we have never even managed to reach a deep understanding of how the video recorder works. Perhaps they have just mistaken an other-worldly sense of the sacred for our tendency to nod off at the slightest opportunity.

Alternatively it could just be that the people who are appointed Archbishops and Popes are just the ones who have managed to outlive all their main rivals for the posts.

But what sort of prayers should a wrinkly say before bedtime and are there any modern alternatives?

Do's And Don'ts Of Saying Your Night-Time Prayers

Do: commence your night time prayers by giving thanks for all the good things that have happened to you during the day.

Don't: commence your night time prayers by screaming the words 'why me?' over and over again at the top of your voice.

Do: use religious language when talking to your God.

Don't: swear or make obscene bodily gestures.

Do: adopt a kneeling position with your hands held together in prayer.

Don't: do star jumps while waving an angry fist at the heavens.

Do: address your God humbly and respectfully.

Don't: use the expression, 'Hey you up there! Are you listening to me, pal?'

Do: share your day's troubles and blessings with your god in a period of quiet meditation before going to bed.

Don't: share your day's troubles and blessings with your neighbours in a period of drunken shouting and swearing from your bedroom window.

Do: make your peace with all those with whom you have disagreed during the day before going to bed.

Don't: challenge them all to a massive fight to the death at dawn.

Do: list the people you want to pray for.

Don't: list all the people you would like God to strike down with botulism.

Things A Wrinkly Has In Common With God

- They are both of a similar age.
- They have both seen many changes during their time.
- They both have quite set ideas about the way things should be in the world.
- Others find it very hard to imagine what could have existed before they came along.
- Fewer people talk to them these days than used to be the case.
- They are both known for being a bit judgemental.
- Both of them avoid direct intervention in current world events if this can possibly be avoided.
- People still turn to them in times of crisis (although in wrinklies' cases this tends to be younger family members looking for a cash hand out).
- Young people are only ever nice to them if they want something in return.
- People often preface things they have to say to them with the words: 'Can you hear me?'
- They have both sent their children out into the world but were not entirely delighted with the reception they were given.
- They both live somewhere nice and peaceful at a bit of a remove from the world.

The Wrinkliest Characters In The Bible

Methuselah

Patriarch mentioned in the Book of Genesis. He lived to the ripe old age of 969 years, this being the oldest age given for any figure in the Bible. Known to many wrinklies today as 'The Kid'.

Adan

Lived to be 950. Like many wrinklies, he had a very nice garden. Unfortunately as a result of meddling by his wrinkly wife, he lost access to this and the pair had to move out (presumably into sheltered accommodation). Even more typically for a wrinkly his kids (Cain and Abel) didn't get on and one of them had to go and live in the Land of Nod (or, for wrinklies, The Land of Nodding Off). Overall Adam and Eve were said to have had 33 sons and 23 daughters. This would obviously have made it a nightmare when they all came to stay at Christmas but luckily for them Christmas hadn't yet been invented.

Noah

Lived to the age of 930. A typical wrinkly male. Keen on DIY, woodwork and collecting an assortment of different pets. Famously had a spot of bother with his local water supplier.

Job

A nipper at just 210 years old. Lost his wealth, his health and his children. The story of many a wrinkly.

Jared

Lived to 962 years old and is thus the second oldest person recorded in the Bible. But who remembers that now? It's all Methuselah this, Methuselah that, isn't it? Jared must have been absolutely gutted. He was pipped to the title of oldest person in the Bible by Methuselah who was just 7 years his senior! Presumably he might have lived that little bit longer if only he'd gone to the gym a bit more often and given up smoking a few years earlier.

Moses

Lived to be 120 and so, in biblical terms, died young. Led his people to the Promised Land without even having to use a sat nav. His wrinkly descendants still complain to this day saying, 'If he'd turned right rather than left when he came out of Egypt, we'd have got the oil!'

Seth

Adam and Eve's third son who lived to be 912 years old. Was born when Adam was 120 years which is a heck of an age to be lumbered with a baby again. Seth's son was born when he was 105 thus further lumbering Adam with babysitting duties when he was 225.

Deborah

At 130, the oldest female wrinkly mentioned in the Bible. Still performing as lead singer of Blondie to this day.

Abraham

Lived to 175 years. It sounds old but it's only 25 in dog years!

Thoughts For Wrinklies To Contemplate

- All you can do in this life is be true to yourself – on the other hand, look where that's got you up to now!

- Laugh and the world laughs with you although the world will probably be thinking, 'What's that idiot laughing for?'

- Learn from your mistakes. If you'd started doing this earlier, you'd be a genius by now!

- It requires more muscles to frown than it does to smile – so frowning will provide you with better exercise.

- Remember, the wrinklies attitude to strangers: there are no strangers in this life, just idiots who haven't annoyed you yet.

- You are what you eat – so after all these years just think what the ingredients list for you must look like.

- If you can keep your head when all those around you are losing theirs, you must be on exceptionally strong medication.

- You learnt all you know today at the school of hard knocks – particularly as regards the best way to treat bruises.

- A smile costs nothing – oh yeah? Tell that to your dentist.

- In the kingdom of the blind, be exceptionally careful when crossing the road no matter what the traffic signal says.

- If you can't think of anything good that happened today, console yourself with this thought: at least it was better than tomorrow's going to be!

Biblical Plagues To Call Down On All Those Who Have Crossed You During The Day

The Bible can be a source of great wisdom and solace for wrinklies. Not only that but it's full of plagues and other fantastic ideas which wrinklies can pray will befall all the people that have annoyed them during the day just gone:

- How about a plague of locusts on the green grocer who sold you that rotten veg this morning?
- For the bin men who emptied rubbish all over your driveway, a plague of flies? After all they left you with one.
- A plague of boils for that sulky supermarket checkout assistant? Oh no. He had already been hit by one, hadn't he?
- And if you see that builder who did that shoddy work for you, get your trumpet out and give him a Jericho-like encounter with the wall he's currently building.
- How about a biblical flood to pour down on the man from the water board who informed you that you still have to pay your bill even though the travellers' camp next door is currently getting its supply from an illegal connection attached to your water meter?
- And the doctor who keeps giving you all that dietary advice can be turned into a pillar of salt (which of course you then won't be allowed to eat).

Oh yes, when wrinklies refer to the Bible there is sure to be a weeping and a gnashing of teeth (or should that be gums).

Chapter 7:
Getting To Sleep And Staying There

Since the dawn of time scientists have been coming up with theories about why we sleep. One of the more popular of these is that it's because we're a bit knackered at the end of the day and there's nothing worth watching on the telly.

But why do we need to sleep at all? Much scientific research has been devoted to this question. Ironically if you try and read any of this, it will quickly make you feel extremely drowsy.

There could be many benefits if we could survive without sleep. For example we would be able to rent out our bedrooms because they weren't being used any more.

Young people seem to need very little sleep. Instead they spend their nights dancing like maniacs at all-night raves while off their faces on Lucozade or Sherbet Dib Dabs (or some similar sort of stimulating substance).

Wrinklies on the other hand are shagged out all the time. You would think that by their time of life, wrinklies would be experts at getting to sleep. Unfortunately they often have great difficulty in doing this. This may partly be due to a lack of physical exercise or poor digestion or alternatively because they are kept awake by the all-night rave organised by the young people living down their street.

Wrinklies can sometimes make getting to sleep look easy but they usually do this while they are watching something they particularly want to see on television.

Prime Minister Mrs Thatcher used to boast to journalists that she hardly slept at all at night, like Dracula. This lack of sleep clearly did her no harm or cause her to lose her grip on reality or develop a pair of bulging red rimmed unblinking eyes.

For most of us though it is important to get a good night's sleep each night and perhaps during the day as well.

Scientists have now identified that our sleeping pattern moves through several cycles. Sleep experts have named these stages rapid eye movement, non-rapid eye movement and dribbling.

The rapid eye movement (or REM) stage is the time when most people dream. The time when wrinklies most often dream is however defined as during any brief lull in a conversation.

Non rapid eye movement is like rapid eye movement but with less rapid eye movement. Wrinklies often experience prolonged periods of non rapid eye movement during the night and periods of non rapid everything else movement during the day.

Sleep is believed to serve a number of cognitive purposes including memory processing. Basically if you don't sleep enough your memory will eventually get so bad that you won't be able to remember where your bedroom is. So potentially it's a vicious circle.

As far as is known, all living animals need to sleep. It is not however advisable to let them all share the bed with you as this will be unhygienic, uncomfortable and the cumulative sound of snoring will be ear shattering.

The Wrinklies Guide To Getting A Good Night's Sleep

Try to relax and let your mind become completely blank – this will become increasingly easy as you get older.

Forget all your earthly desires – again this will become increasingly easy as you get older.

Don't do anything in bed that might suddenly raise your heart rate – this is getting a bit repetitive now isn't it?

Empty your mind of all thought – this can usually be achieved by watching anything broadcast on television during the prime time schedule.

Achieving a restful state can also be helped by having a nice bedtime drink – a mug full of a hot milky beverage should do the trick although a few cans of something stronger can also reduce you to a condition of complete rest fairly quickly (or possibly to a condition of complete paralysis which is quite similar).

Consider all the good things that have happened to you during the day just gone – don't start feeling sorry for yourself when you realize the highlight of your day was the chocolate HobNob you had with your elevenses.

Stroking a pet may also help reduce your stress levels and heart rate – it will also reduce your breathing rate if the animal settles down for the night on your face shortly after you've nodded off.

Wrinklies Theories of Sleep

We need to sleep each night because our body needs a period of time to rest and recuperate after the exertions and stresses of the day. This is a brilliant theory but obviously someone should tell your body about it.

Unfortunately the theory doesn't explain why your body decides to keep you keep awake each night by fidgeting, making odd noises and requiring numerous visits to the toilet.

You need to rest each night to allow your body to repair and rejuvenate itself so you stay looking healthy and young. One glance at yourself in the mirror would suggest that you can't ever have slept a wink in your life.

Overall you spend about a third of your life asleep. So if you haven't had quite enough sleep so far there is a genuine danger you may suddenly drop off and keep snoring away for an entire decade or two.

In your dreams you are able to do all sorts of outrageous and incredible things that you could never do in real life. This is why wrinklies spend most nights dreaming of repeatedly bending over and touching their toes.

You sleep to restore order and balance to your mind and body. Well, you would if your bed didn't have that wonky leg.

There are many theories of why we sleep but no-one knows the real reason.

In fact now you've started thinking about it, the problem is probably going to keep you awake all night!

Wrinklies' Dreams And What They Mean

Everyone is fascinated by dreams aren't they? Everyone, that is, with the small exception of everyone else on the planet who didn't have the dream themselves.

So in other words, everyone is fascinated by their own dreams but extremely bored by everyone else's. In fact if someone starts telling you about the amazing dream they had last night, it will probably be so boring it will send you straight off to sleep.

This does however mean that the moment they shut up about their dream, you can wake up and get your own back by telling them about the dream you yourself were just having as a result of being bored to death by their dream.

The imagery of dreams was analysed by the celebrated bald, bearded wrinkly Sigmund Freud. Freud was the father of psychoanalysis and also of several children (the majority of whom were also bald and bearded).

Freud believed that our dreams are all about wish fulfilment, although eating too much cheese before bedtime may come into it as well.

Freud published his book *The Interpretation of Dreams* in 1899. This was a 500-page tome in which Freud expressed his theory of why we dream. In fact the book just has the words, 'It's all about sex innit?' printed on every page. Or was that just in one particularly poorly translated edition that was quickly withdrawn from sale?

But do wrinklies' dreams mean exactly the same as they would to a normal person?

Dream Image Or Event	What It Signifies To A Normal Person	What It Signifies To A Wrinkly
Flying	Sex	I must check if there's any package holiday bargains on the internet at the moment!
Water	Sex	Perhaps a cruise would be nice instead!
Falling	Yet more sex	Maybe I should get one of those emergency alarm buttons to go round my neck!
Lighthouse	Phallic symbol of a sexual nature	I must remember to buy some new light bulbs from the supermarket tomorrow!
Bushes	Full frontal sex	Time to spray the rhododendrons!
Entering a tunnel	Let's face it – it's sex again isn't it?	Has my Senior Citizens' Railcard run out?
Nudity in a public place	Sexual desire, exhibitionism, sex, sex, sex and more sex	Damn it! I took all my clothes off again when I went to the shopping centre this morning didn't I?
Sex	Hugely perverse kinky sex	I really must write a letter of complaint to the *Daily Mail* about that filthy television programme I saw on BBC2 last night!

Things A Wrinkly Can Count To Help Get Off To Sleep (If You Want To Irritate Yourself)

- The number of times you have been asked to participate in a telephone survey during the past week.
- The number of times petrol has gone up in price over the past few days.
- The number of youths you have seen over the past week with their trousers half way down their backsides exhibiting a couple of inches of their Calvin Klein underpants in the process.
- The number of pills prescribed by the doctor that you have to take every day.
- The number of charity collection bags you have had stuffed through your letter box in the past week.
- The number of buttons you have to press in order to speak to a human being when you call your bank.
- The number of advertising leaflets that fall out of your TV guide when you pick it up.
- The number of TV cookery shows you have seen in the past 24 hours.
- Your wrinkly friends coming up to you one by one to tell you about their latest health problem.
- The number of individual aches and pains you have flashing around your wrinkly old body.

Things A Wrinkly Can Count To Help Get Off To Sleep (If You Want Something A Little More Entertaining)

- Flashy sports cars being overtaken on the dual carriageway by you in your old banger.
- Cold-calling salesmen coming to your front door and being electrocuted when they press your specially booby-trapped doorbell.
- Politicians losing their parliamentary seats on election night.
- Bankers being lined up and told one by one that they are going to lose their annual bonuses.
- Hoodies being given ASBOs.
- Bits dropping off the house of an irritating neighbour.
- Simon Cowell being repeatedly kneed in the groin by every *X Factor* auditionee he's ever been rude to.
- Telling all your unwanted telephone callers to bugger off one after the other!
- All the 4x4s in the neighbourhood going into a pile up on the local dual carriageway.
- Local troublemakers being chased by their own pit bull terriers.
- A highly tattooed upstart of a celebrity having his tattoos removed one by one with an industrial sander.

Counting Wrinkly Sheep: The Best Way To Get To Sleep... Or Is It?

Counting sheep is a method frequently used by those wanting to get off to sleep. There is however little or no evidence that this system really works. After all:

- Are shepherds notorious for falling asleep after a few minutes surveying their herds?
- At livestock auctions, do the auctioneer and spectators pass out as soon as a few sheep walk round the ring in front of them?
- When performing surgical procedures in hospital operating theatres, do doctors ever attempt to put their patients to sleep with a brief demonstration by a recent winner from the TV series *One Man And His Dog*?
- When a stage hypnotist wishes to put someone into a deep sleep, doesn't he usually dangle a pocket watch in front of them... not a sheep!

There is however one thing worse than counting sheep and that is counting wrinklies. Yes, you have probably seen so many of your fellow wrinklies during the day that their balding or blue rinsed images are now permanently burnt into your mind.

However counting these wrinklies attempting to jump over a five-bar gate will not help you get to sleep. Instead you will lie awake all night working yourself up into an apoplectic rage while muttering, 'Jump, you stupid old wrinkly! What's the matter with you? It's only a small gate! You'll never get over it shuffling at that speed! Put your Zimmer frame down and jump!'

Wrinklies' Night Time Fantasies

The Tropical Island

You find yourself washed up on the shore of an idyllic tropical island where the beautiful and naked inhabitants are all eager to do anything at all for anyone who can bring them up to date on the latest events in Coronation Street, Eastenders and/or The Archers.

The New Neighbour

A new, highly attractive, young neighbour moves in next door to you. You invite them round for afternoon tea and are surprised to discover that for them Werther's Originals seem to have a strong aphrodisiac quality.

The Celebrity

You receive an unexpected call asking you to re-pot some geraniums for a top celebrity after whom you have always secretly lusted. The celebrity returns home and discovers you in their garden shed. Seeing you with your sleeves rolled up, up to your arms in potting compost, they suddenly become unable to control themselves.

The Most Romantic City In The World

You meet a gorgeous young member of the opposite sex who tells you that their dream has always been to see the sights of Paris while sitting on the back of a mobility scooter.

Save The World

Humanity is doomed unless scientists can find an aged person who can teach young people how to make love properly again.

How To Tell Your Dreams From Reality

You are trying to run away because someone is chasing you, but find it difficult to make your legs move.

Experiencing difficulty in moving your legs while running is a common element in many peoples' dreams. For wrinklies it is also a common element in reality, particularly if you have just got up out of a chair a bit too quickly.

The clincher is the fact that someone is taking the trouble to chase you. If you are being chased by a scantily clad member of the opposite sex, it is probably all a dream. If however you are being chased by someone wanting you to switch your gas and electricity supplier, it is probably reality.

You are naked in a public place.

Are you feeling chilly and can you hear the sound of giggling and/or sirens approaching in the distance? If so, it's reality so put your cardie back on quick!

The Queen has come to your house for tea.

This was once said to have been a commonly experienced dream. It is of course unlikely that Her Majesty would wander into your house unannounced and demand you get the PG Tips and HobNobs out. On the other hand, she's getting on a bit herself so maybe she does stroll into peoples' houses in a state of confusion. Better get the best china ready but avoid giving her an old chipped mug issued to commemorate any of her children's failed marriages.

You discover that you unexpectedly have to sit an extremely difficult exam paper for which you have done no preparation.

This is another common dream. Congratulations if you ever have it! You could lie in bed at night recalling your happy childhood memories: the long hot summers, having fun with your friends, your first ever kiss...

But no!

Instead you've decided to have a dream about everyone's least favourite part of childhood: going into a dingy great hall, sitting trembling at a desk and spending three hours sweating like a pig while attempting to do an exam on a subject you have no interest in or knowledge about whatsoever.

It might however be worth checking the exam paper you see in front of you. If a glance at the top of the paper reveals that it is not an exam after all but a tax return or a passport application form, bad luck! It's probably grim reality once again!

You are in a large building desperately trying to find where the toilets are located.

This is a common dream. It is also how we wrinklies spend every minute of the day once we leave the comfort of our own homes.

There is therefore very little possibility of being able to tell whether this is a dream or reality other than to find and use the toilet facilities.

If you later discover your bed sheets are damp, it was a dream.

Lullabies for Wrinklies

'Rock-a-bye Wrinkly'

Rock-a-bye wrinkly, in the tree top,
When the wind blows, the wrinkly will drop,
Down comes the wrinkly and suffers a thoracic disorder,
All because he tried to prune his own leylandii border.

'All Through The Night'

Out of bed and along to the toilet,
All through the night,
Tramping downstairs, turn the kettle on and boil it,
All through the night.
One more cup of tea to help quench your thirst,
All through the night,
Lying back in bed with a bladder fit to burst,
All through the night.

'Hush Little Wrinkly'

Hush little wrinkly, don't say a word
Mama's gonna buy you some lemon curd
And if that lemon curd don't taste
Mama's gonna buy you some curry paste.

And if that curry tastes like stew
Mama's gonna buy you a vindaloo
And if that vindaloo ain't strong
We're all gonna know your tastebuds have gone.

'Hinkly Wrinkly'

Hinkly Wrinkly sat on a wall,
Hinkly Wrinkly had a great fall,
A lawyer took the wrinkly as one of his cases,
And sued the wall's owner on a no-win-no-fee basis.

'Wrinkle, Wrinkle Little Pa'

Wrinkle, wrinkle little Pa
How I wonder what you are
Sitting in your favourite chair
Without a tooth or single hair.

Up above, your hand held high
A Double Diamond helps time fly
Wrinkle wrinkle little Pa
In your favourite corner of the bar.

'Silent Night'

Silent night, noiseless night
The snoring cure has turned out right
Up each nostril there's a plug
You're so quiet I could give you a hug
'cos I can sleep in pee – eace
At last I can sleep in peace.

Silent night, blissful night
Not a sound since we turned out the light
Though you're now verging on comatose
You can't have died I suppose?
But if you have I can be sure – ure
It's the last I'll hear of your snore.

Chapter 8:
Can't Sleep?

What should you do if you can't sleep? This is the terrible problem many of us face every single day. And it's even worse if it happens while you're lying in bed at night.

There are a range of sleep disorders to choose from these days. These include insomnia, sleep apnea or depression, delayed sleep phase syndrome and not being able to get comfy.

Wrinklies can have difficulty sleeping as a result of many different things. In fact wrinklies are endlessly inventive as regards things that will keep them awake at night.

A wrinkly can be kept awake by any one or any combination of the following:

> any twitch, itch or pulse anywhere about their own person; the sound of their own breathing; any aches or pains they have; the slightest movement, snoring or sharp inhalation of breath made by their wrinkly bed companion; the need to go to the toilet (either now or within the next few hours); pets moving about anywhere in the house; noises produced by the central heating system; any creaks, squeaks or odd noises; people anywhere nearby communicating in anything more than a whisper; any vehicle driving past; any television or music being played nearby at any volume; young people doing anything at all; a firework going off anywhere within a 20-mile radius;

murderers smashing their way in through the French
windows downstairs, etc.

Yes, you name it – a wrinkly will be kept awake by it.

If they gave out prizes for innovation in the field of
insomnia, wrinklies would sweep the board.

Wrinklies are the world experts at not being able to get
sleep. They have lived so long that they know everything
that can possibly keep them awake. And if these things
don't happen, wrinklies will instead lie there worrying that
they're about to happen at any moment.

Basically we wrinklies almost never get a wink of sleep.
This explains a lot about our appearance and character.
Anyone who got as little sleep as we do would look and
act like a wrinkly. They would be grumpy, they would
have bags under their eyes and they would spend their
days moaning about everything.

Also of course, wrinklies have lived so long that they
now have particular expectations of sleep. They refuse to
be fobbed off with any old sleep. Wrinklies demand a good
sleep. They need a proper night's sleep. They want top
quality, luxury, Taste The Difference sleep every night of
the week.

And if they don't get it, they will give everyone they
meet the next day a detailed critique of the disappointing
sleep they had.

So how can a wrinkly make sure of getting a good
night's sleep without disturbance?

Do they need to invest in earplugs, eye masks and
enough drugs to sedate an elephant?

Or is it too much to ask that the rest of humanity could
just try to stay quiet for a few hours every night?

Things Wrinklies Should Try Not To Think About At Bedtime

Things That You Should Avoid Thinking About At Bedtime	Why You Shouldn't Worry
The thought that the house might burn down in the night	No need to panic. You perform an impromptu test of your smoke alarm every day when you make a piece of toast... or has doing that worn out the batteries?
The threat of burglars and murderers breaking into the house in the middle of the night	No need to worry! You've got so many locks and security fittings on all the doors and windows they could never possibly get in! Of course, if they've already managed to slip in during the day while you weren't looking, you'll never manage to get the door unlocked in time to escape!
The scary programme that you have just watched on TV before going to bed (e.g. a documentary about health, the news or *Crimewatch* – which always rubs it in with its final message directed specifically at wrinkly viewers: 'don't have nightmares!')	Don't worry! It's only the television! It's not real! Oh no, hang on! The news, a documentary, *Crimewatch*! It is all real!! Panic!!!
That other scary thing you saw just before bedtime	In future remember not to look downwards when climbing out of the bath

The trauma that results from being told that an acquaintance is not well or even not long for this world	Now you're a wrinkly you'll hear this kind of thing every single day of your life! You'll soon get used to it and instead of being traumatic, it will become a source of endless fascination
The fear of an earthquake occurring in the middle of the night	Well, it's been a while since you've had the opportunity to ask your partner, 'Did the earth move for you?'
The worry that the chimney stack will fall over through the roof and down on top of your bed during the night	Don't be ridiculous! That chimney stack has been standing there since before you were born...! Oops! Maybe it would be best to move the bed a few inches to the right. Or alternatively, switch sides with your spouse whenever it's windy
The thought of dying in your sleep	Look on the bright side! If this happens you'll get a really good lie-in in the morning
The fear that your house might be haunted	You have now lived so long, you are probably older than most ghosts. Any ghosts will probably therefore be more scared of you as well as looking slightly healthier

Composing Imaginary Ripostes And Letters Of Complaint

Why do so many of us wrinklies start mentally composing imaginary ripostes and letters of complaint when we go to bed? Why does the part of us that is most grumpy and quick to take offence wake up when the rest of our wrinkly old bodies are trying to get to sleep?

Once this grumpy bit of us wakes up, it starts analysing all the impertinences and lack of consideration we have encountered from others during the day.

These didn't bother us at the time. At the time we remained polite and calm in our dealings with the series of ill-mannered buffoons life found to throw at us.

They came to us during the past 24 hours doing, saying and/or emailing the most incredibly annoying things. But then, as we wrinklies know, that is what other people have been put on this Earth to do.

When our wrinkly heads hit the pillow however, the irritable little person inside us wakes up.

This little fellow inside our heads spends hours during the night examining the maddening things people have said and done during the day just gone. He then goes on to painstakingly work out carefully worded responses that, come the new day, we should give or send to those who have vexed us.

This then is the process of composing imaginary ripostes and letters of complaint! It is one of the most efficient ways available to stop wrinklies getting off to sleep easily.

You lie for hours in bed devising arguments so carefully and brilliantly worded that, hearing them, those who annoyed you over the past 24 hours would immediately see the error of their ways and fall to their knees begging you to pardon their foolishness.

But it's a waste of time! You're in bed! All the idiots who tormented you during the day have gone away!

Apart that is from one of them!

A wrinkly bed companion may be lying close at hand. This makes them ideally placed to receive your complaints and withering put down lines as soon as you think of them (and whether or not they were the ones who provoked them in the first place).

Otherwise you have to commit everything to memory and type up your letters of outrage and complaint in the morning. You can try typing them in bed but this really will keep you and your partner awake.

Perhaps what we wrinklies need is some sort of computerised dictation program wired up to our beds. This would transcribe our nocturnal pronouncements as we angrily mutter them from our pillows.

Ideally this program would then go on to put our night-time rants into emails which it would then automatically dispatch to their intended recipients.

By the time we woke up in the morning those who had annoyed us during the day just gone would have our full and frank assessment of their behaviour waiting for them in their in-boxes.

What could possibly go wrong?

Things You Should Really Try Not To Worry About While You're Lying In Bed

Money problems

There's no use lying awake worrying about this. There's not much you can do to make money while you're in bed is there? OK there is one thing but that sort of career change is probably inadvisable at your time of life.

The weight you've put on

Are you lying awake worrying that you've put on weight? Well, try and get to sleep and dream that you're out jogging! Of course this sort of weight loss regime will probably be more successful if you jog while you're awake and then spend all night dreaming of eating cakes. On the other hand, as we all know, if you do dream you're eating a big cake, you will wake up in the morning to find that your pillow has mysteriously disappeared. If however you are worrying about the weight you have put on and you are unable to sleep because your bed keeps collapsing, your worries may have some justification.

Losing your looks

This is never going to be a problem when you're asleep. Think about it. What's the worst that can happen? You'll dream you're making an advance on a gorgeous member of the opposite sex only for them to rebuff you with the words, 'In your dreams!' You can then respond quick as a flash, 'Exactly!' This will leave them with no choice but to fall into your arms.

Getting older

You should not worry about getting older while you're asleep. We're all getting older and we're all doing this at roughly the same rate as each other: one second per second.

It is therefore very unlikely that you will go to bed looking beautiful and young and wake up in the morning looking hideous and old. This does occasionally happen in the following situations: you go to bed caked in lots of make up which all comes off in the night; you go to bed and the plastic surgeon whose bill you haven't paid breaks into your house in the night and removes his handiwork; you stay asleep for several decades.

Most of these ways to age suddenly and terribly in the night are fairly unlikely to happen although a similar effect can also be achieved by the following method: look at yourself in the mirror without your glasses on immediately before going to bed and then in the morning look at yourself with your glasses on.

Dying in your sleep

What are you worried about? Waking up, finding yourself dead and the shock being almost enough to kill you?

What you should be worried about is falling into such a deep sleep that people can't tell the difference and decide to bury you anyway. It is therefore always a good idea to keep your mobile phone in your pyjama pocket at night. Then in an emergency you can phone someone to come and dig you back up again.

Wrinkly Ghosties And Wrinkly Ghoulies

Skeletal figures, ghastly pale faces and constant wailing. That's wrinklies for you.

But what about the ghostly apparitions that might be found in a run down spooky old house. Could they be wrinklies as well?

Evidence seems to exist that ghosts are in fact all wrinklies. Well, they spend their time hanging round in run-down, old houses don't they?

Ghostly wrinklies walking through the walls

These are believed to be the spirits of wrinklies who died unable to find their spectacles and who are now doomed to wander the earth in a state of myopic confusion and frustration unable to find either the door frame or their car keys.

The headless wrinkly

These figures are often seen holding their decapitated heads under their arms. Some say they are the ghosts of wrinklies who died after making an over forceful attempt to correct a crick in the neck that had developed during the night. Alternatively they may be the ghosts of wrinkly men who were desperate to examine the bald spot on the back of their heads in closer detail.

A ghostly figure looking in through the window

Clearly the ghost of a wrinkly who has forgotten to take his/her keys when they went out of the front door.

Poltergeists

They go round the house smashing crockery. They are undoubtedly the spirits of wrinklies attempting to carry a tray of tea things from the kitchen to the living room.

The sound of chains rattling and moaning

The ghost of a wrinkly who has died on the toilet and who then spends the rest of eternity moaning that there isn't a fresh roll of toilet paper handy.

Is anybody there?

When conducting séances, a medium will often have to call, 'Is anybody there?' several times before a reply is received from the spirit world. This suggests that the spirits must be slightly deaf and therefore quite possibly wrinkly as well.

Ghostly knocking on the walls

This is the sound produced by a wrinkly ghost checking his cavity wall insulation during the middle of the night.

A shrouded ghostly figure

A ghostly figure in a white sheet? Is it a rubber sheet? If so it could be the ghost of an incontinent wrinkly.

Weird noises in the middle of the night

The ghost of a wrinkly with tummy trouble.

Terrifying Wrinkly Nightmares And Explanations To Help Put Your Mind At Rest

Wrinkly nightmare	Possible explanation
The sound of ominous creaking somewhere in the house	It's your own creaking old bones moving as you breathe in and out
The sound of an eerie wind blowing	Again you probably don't have to to look very far for the source of this
A strange distant disembodied voice calling your name over and over again in the darkness	You forgot to hang up the phone earlier after calling your cousin in Australia, didn't you?
Weird ethereal coloured lights floating just outside your window and shining in through your curtains	You haven't got round to taking down the Christmas decorations this year
The sound of someone moving around downstairs in the middle of the night	You live in a flat
The silhouette of a small devil with pointed ears sitting at the end of your bed looking at you	You shouldn't let the cats sleep in the bedroom with you
Slow ominous footsteps coming up the stairs towards you	Your spouse is turning in for the night at last
Heavy breathing in the darkness as though from some strange and terrible brutish creature	Your spouse has managed to get up the stairs, into bed and is now lying next to you
A light appearing above your head and a ladder descending towards you	Your spouse has got up again in the night and, in a moment of confusion, has gone up to into the attic

Bad Bedtime Habits For Wrinklies

If a wrinkly wishes to enjoy a good night's sleep, the following activities may be inadvisable just before bedtime:

- Calling everyone you know and leaving messages on their answer phones to call you back no matter what time they get in;
- Giving yourself a night-time treat of a family size pack of liquorice novelties washed down with a flagon of prune juice;
- Making an attempt on the world record for the number of barrels of water a single individual can drink in under an hour;
- Inviting a suspected local serial killer round for a nightcap and then telling him to see himself out when he's finished;
- Partaking in an extensive late night espresso coffee sampling session;
- Renting your spare room out as rehearsal space for the thrash metal band formed by members of the local insomniacs self help group;
- Practicing your fire eating act while sitting in bed;
- Conjuring up some evil sprits using your handy bedside ouija board set;
- Unnecessarily raising your heart rate by going up the stairs to bed as fast as you can on a pogo stick followed by half an hour's trampoline practice on your mattress.

Chapter 9:
Wrinkly Bed Companions

Wrinklies may not share their beds quite as often or with quite as many companions as the oversexed younger generation. On the other hand wrinklies do have their own bed companions. There is often a wrinkly partner and possibly a wrinkly pet hidden somewhere about the bedding. This means that many wrinklies can still boast to their friends that they enjoy a threesome every night!

But when you get to our time of life, the attractions of sharing your bed with others are perhaps less obvious. It's difficult enough to get to sleep with your own wrinkly old body twitching, fidgeting and sniffling away all night while accompanying the whole performance with a series of peculiar noises. If you've got a second wrinkly body crammed in next to yours doing the same thing, isn't that twice the amount of distraction?

Ever since that bloke broke into the queen's bedroom at Buckingham Palace in the 1980s, we have known that Her Maj and her husband don't sleep together. Presumably Prince Philip was being kept awake each night by the sound of his wife's crown on the pillow next to him tinkling away as she breathed deeply in her royal sleep.

Nevertheless there are probably lots of reasons why other wrinklies should continue to share their beds.

Obviously one of the main reasons you still share a bed with your wrinkly partner is for all those long nights filled with non-stop, rampant, passionate sex. No, thought not.

Like many wrinklies you perfected the art of lovemaking years ago, didn't you? That's why you decided to retire from this art form when you were still on top (as it were) and leave your wrinkly partner with unspoilt memories of ultimate ecstasy.

Besides if you tried that sort of thing, think of the appalling squeaking noises that would be produced. And your bedstead would probably make a bit of a racket as well.

No, these days if any of your friends tell you they're a 'bit of a five times a night man', this probably just refers to the number of nocturnal visits they make to the bathroom.

You could say that by sharing a bed, you help keep each other warm at night. Unfortunately even this isn't true any more. These days your circulation is so bad, you and your partner keep each other cold at night and set each other shivering if either of you accidentally comes into contact with the other's ice cold extremities.

But at least it should be possible for you to demonstrate enduring affection with a brief cuddle. Unless, that is, one of you then experiences a sudden hot flush which leaves the pair of you sweating and gasping for breath at opposite ends of your steaming mattress.

But what makes the ideal wrinkly bed companion? What is it that we do to annoy them and is there anything else we can do to make sure that we get the bed all to ourselves?

Celebrity Bed Companions And Why They Wouldn't Suit A Female Wrinkly

Tom Cruise	You'd be kept awake all night by the light reflecting off his great pearly teeth
Russell Brand	He's probably not going to come up to bed at a sensible time is he?
Mick Jagger	When you're a wrinkly, the last thing you want in your bed is someone with extra wrinkles to spare – on the plus side he would make you look quite young
David Beckham	Presumably if you wanted to sit and read, he'd just sit there stuck for something to do
Simon Cowell	Just think of the critical comments you'll get for the cup of cocoa you took him
Arnold Schwarzenegger	Every single time he went to the toilet during the night, he'd tell you, 'I'll be back!'
Andy Murray	He moans, he grunts, he shouts and swears – it would be just like spending the night with your usual wrinkly old bed partner
Ant & Dec	A bit small – we suppose you could use one as a pillow and the other as a hot water bottle
Russell Crowe	He'd definitely get a bit cross if you stole the covers off him
Tom Jones	The wrinkly female's ideal man – but if that's the way he sounds when he sings, imagine what his snoring must be like
Prince William	He's probably a nice young man but he won't be used to putting the cat out and making sure the back door's locked himself, will he?

Celebrity Bed Companions And Why They Wouldn't Suit A Male Wrinkly

Kylie Minogue	Too small – you'd keep losing her in the duvet
Madonna	Too muscular – if you get into a pillow fight with her, you're very unlikely to win
Jordan	It will be cheaper just to buy yourself a new pair of big pillows
Posh Spice	Too small a surface area to plant your feet on so you can warm them up on a cold night
Britney Spears	All very nice I'm sure but is she going to take turns to make a nice cup of tea in the morning?
Mariah Carey	Unlikely to be satisfied by your electric blanket and teasmade
Any supermodel	If you try and cuddle up to them in bed they will snap in half plus they will never make you a decent fry-up for breakfast
Nigella Lawson	The perfect bed companion for a male wrinkly except for the fact you would never get to bed because you'd permanently be in the kitchen stuffing yourself on her cooking
Joanna Lumley	Again a wrinkly's ideal but if you get involved with her the Ghurkhas will surely be after your guts for garters
Angelina Jolie	Just imagine the cold sniffy look she will give you when she sees you in your tartan design pyjamas
Lady Gaga	She is bound to take up more than her fair share of space in your wardrobe

How To Avoid Upsetting Your Wrinkly Partner In Bed

Don't steal the bedclothes

Who says wrinklies don't get enough exercise? Wrinkly couples spend many nights playing tug-of-war with one another. This is played in the wrinkly couple's sleep using the duvet in place of a rope. This game of physical skill is played by wrinklies during much of the colder periods of the year (which to wrinklies usually means the entire year apart from the first week of August).

No, nothing annoys your partner more than having their bed covers stolen during the night. Even heaving them to one side in order to fit a younger more attractive companion next to you in their stead will annoy them less.

After a certain age they will regard this not so much as an affront to their dignity than as an extra source of warmth during the cold winter nights (n.b. the authors cannot accept legal responsibility if you choose to follow this advice and then discover your partner's reaction is not quite as described).

However if they wake up and find themselves lying exposed to the Arctic wind blowing through your bedroom and suffering the first symptoms of frostbite while you are wrapped up in the entire duvet like an enormous sausage roll, they are likely to be displeased.

You should also particularly avoid stealing the bedclothes from your partner if they are now estranged from you and live in a different house to which you do not have legitimate access.

Don't warm your feet on your partner's back

During the day wrinkly wives will frequently complain to their wrinkly husbands that they feel less supple than they used to. After the passage of years their joints are now painful and stiff and are difficult to bend.

During the night though, it's a completely different story.

Suddenly a wrinkly woman's leg joints become as flexible as those of a 20-year-old. This flexibility is not of course exhibited as part of any pleasurable bed-based activities.

No, instead the wrinkly husband discovers that his wrinkly wife's joints have been mysteriously rejuvenated when he becomes aware that she has managed to lift her legs right up in order to plant her freezing cold feet flat on his back.

Often a wrinkly man will have a permanent imprint of a pair of size 6 feet on his back. This marking has been indelibly left by a process similar to the freeze branding of identification marks on farm animals.

Why do wrinkly women's feet go cold from the 1st of September until the following May? Perhaps it is the first sign of the changing seasons. Perhaps it is because these days her feet spend much of the day shaded from direct sunlight. No-one really knows.

So, wrinkly men, this is the real reason your partner prepares a nice hot drink for you just before bedtime. As far as they are concerned what they are doing is filling up their hot water bottle for the night.

Don't keep your partner awake all night by snoring

A wrinkly may not care for the noises (verbal or otherwise) that emanate from their wrinkly partner during the daytime. During the night however they will find themselves subjected to a sonic performance that is even less welcome.

Wrinklies will often spend much of the night producing some of the most disgusting noises to have ever emerged from the upper half of a living creature. During the hours of darkness they will lie producing a bizarre low frequency rumbling. This is accompanied by the sound of gargling and guttural oscillation from various parts of their internal tubing.

The whole effect is akin to lying in the middle of a swamp full of bullfrogs and walruses, several of whom seem to be performing Swedish massages on each other. If your central heating system were making this racket each night, you'd apply for a boiler scrappage payment after evacuating the building for health and safety purposes.

You might assume that the noise if not the physical vibration produced by this aural extravaganza would be sufficient to wake everyone in the vicinity including the wrinkly producing it. But no! The wrinkly responsible for this soundscape sleeps on completely oblivious of his or her guttural dexterity.

Various devices can now be used to reduce the sound of snoring. A clip over the nose may help. Or, if you want a more permanent solution, try several very strong clips over the nose, nostrils and mouth.

The Dangers Of Multiple Wrinklies In One Bed – A Wrinkly Physicist Explains

The presence of one wrinkly man and his wrinkly wife lying in bed together inevitably means a lot of wrinkles in a small confined space. This is particularly the case if their sheets and blankets are also quite wrinkly.

The possibility then exists for all the hundreds perhaps thousands of individual wrinkles contained together in the bed to combine during the night. This can eventually lead to the formation of what scientists describe as a super-massive black wrinkle.

This resulting cosmologically huge wrinkle would be so enormous it would be capable of drawing everything in the surrounding area into itself.

It's a wonder that wrinkly couples don't wake up in the morning to discover that their bedside cabinets, their bedside lamps, their teasmade, dressing table and entire double bed have all disappeared as a result of being consumed by a super-massive wrinkle in the night.

This is the real reason why wrinklies can't find items such as their slippers or glasses when they wake up.

The super massive wrinkle would potentially affect all space and time around it. This is why wrinklies' bedrooms often have a retro look and seem to be filled with items dating from some lost period of time.

Even at the border of the region of space surrounding the wrinkly bed there will be an effect and the walls will be decorated with wallpaper which appears to have come from a previous century.

The Wrinkly Sutra

Positions for wrinklies to adopt in bed to help ensure that hanky panky is not only unlikely but probably physically impossible as well!

The Missionary Position

The lady wrinkly lies flat on the bed waiting while the gentleman wrinkly sits downstairs in the living room with the vicar who has unexpectedly popped by for a chat and a cup of tea.

The Doggie Position

The gentleman wrinkly lies facing upwards on one side of the bed. The lady wrinkly lies facing upwards on the other side of the bed. Directly between the gentleman wrinkly and the lady wrinkly lies their great hairy pet Labrador snoring away contentedly.

The Sixty-Nine Position

As everyone knows this position gets its name from a reference to a Chinese takeaway menu. After enjoying a takeaway earlier in the evening, the gentleman wrinkly and the lady wrinkly bend over. This is because they are now not feeling well and are both poised over the toilet bowl.

The Spoons Position

The gentleman wrinkly and the lady wrinkly both bend over the cutlery drawer and engage in several minutes hard polishing with the Brasso.

The Lotus Position

This is not advisable for wrinklies. The Ford Focus Position, the Vauxhall Astra Position and the Rover 200 Position may all be better suited to wrinklies but probably not the Lotus Position.

Suspended Congress

The gentleman wrinkly stands with his back to the lady wrinkly and begins talking to her. When he turns round he discovers that his lady wrinkly partner must have left the room a little while ago and that he has therefore been talking to himself for the last ten minutes.

The Golden Shower

The gentleman wrinkly returns home and discovers that his lady wrinkly partner has had an ostentatious new bathroom suite installed without his knowledge.

Annual Sex

Frequently subject of a very unfortunate misprint in a number of widely available sex manuals. As wrinklies know it should of course really be 'annual sex'.

Karma Suture

A sexual position in which things go disastrously wrong thereby resulting in the need for immediate surgical treatment.

Karma Chameleon

Being put off sex by the thought of Boy George.

The Wrinkly's Guide To Why Sex Is An Overrated Pastime

- Anything that young people like can't be much good.

- Everyone is obsessed with sex these days but general election results show how misguided the majority view can be.

- Sex was all right back in the good old days (when the wrinkly's generation invented it) but the over exposure it gets now has spoilt it for everyone.

- Sex was specifically invented to produce other people. And if there's one thing that irritates wrinklies it's other people!

- Modern day sex seems to involve a lot of moaning. Wrinklies are capable of moaning but with much less fuss and effort.

- There are plenty of more constructive ways for a wrinkly to put his or her back out.

- For wrinklies it's a bit like the pop music of their youth. It's probably still fun but the equipment necessary to enjoy it may require some servicing or a complete upgrade.

- Sadly it is necessary for wrinklies to avoid any strenuous bed based activities these days as the guarantee on their mattress has probably run out.

- A wrinkly can get quite enough sex for one day just by reading a magazine or newspaper or by watching an evening's television.

- Two words to sum up why wrinklies and sex shouldn't go together: Peter Stringfellow.

Here Are Some More Bed Companions For You

Even wrinklies who sleep alone get to share their bed. And not in a particularly nice way!

A used mattress may contain anywhere between 100,000 to 10 million dust mites. So looking on the positive side, you should never be lonely at night.

According to the *Wall Street Journal*, 'The average mattress will double its weight in ten years as a result of being filled with dust mites and their detritus.'

And do you know what these dust mites are feeding away on? Yes, on you!

These miniature bed companions spend their lives chomping away at dead skin cells. Dead skin cells are of course what wrinklies are mainly made up of. So when a wrinkly climbs into bed, there's a good chance they might be completely eaten away during the night by their own mattress.

If you wake up in the morning and find your wrinkly partner has disappeared listen very carefully. You may hear their muffled call for help from within your mattress. They may have been dragged inside the mattress by 10 million dust mites who were all feeling a bit peckish.

If your mattress has turned man (or wrinkly) eater it may be time to get a nice new one. If your wrinkly partner is still trapped inside you could release them before taking the old mattress to the tip.

Or you might just like to get a nice new partner to go with your nice new mattress.

Chapter 10: Wrinkly Wresolutions

You might think that at a certain time of life – all right, let's spell it out: wrinkliehood – you wouldn't need to make any more resolutions, or even wresolutions.

All that stuff's for younger people. People who still feel they've got something to prove. Wrinklies however, have been there, done that and got the wrinkled T-shirt.

But that's where you'd be wrong.

Wrinklies have to keep on top of things. You may be retired, you may have finally got the kids off your hands, but there are a thousand and one things to occupy your time.

In fact, you wonder how you ever found the time to fit in a job and a family and all that other stuff.

From the moment a wrinkly wakes up and has to make their first decision of the day (tea in bed, tea at the breakfast table, or tea in the garden), to the last one at night(cocoa, Ovaltine, or perhaps something a little stronger) it's go, go, go.

The first peek through the bedroom curtains presents the wrinkly with a multitude of choices too.

Has that flipping paperboy chucked the newspaper in the porch again like some dreadful American child from a 1950s sitcom? Have the dustmen left half the rubbish strewn behind them like participants in a wastepaper chase? Have the sparrows been at my silvertop again?

Already the wrinkly is writing imaginary letters of

complaint. Already the blood, which has simmered down overnight to a lukewarm sludge, has begun to boil.

Oh yes, and this is before the sun is barely over the horizon.

And then there are the health issues. The wrinkly wakes to find a strange stiffness in the left knee joint. That wasn't there yesterday, says the wrinkly to him or herself. Let's see if it passes before I make a doctor's appointment.

That twinge in my tooth – how can it be? It's a crown for goodness sake. That strange lump on the back of my hand – has it always been there? Oh yes, here's one just the same on the other hand. That's all right then.

Then there are the hundred and one decisions of what to do today. Do I need to renew my library books? Oh God, they've changed the system at the library to self-service and I don't know whether I can go through that again.

Should I speak to the next-door neighbour about their cat doing its business in my vegetable patch? How many times do I have to explain to them that cat poo is not manure? Perhaps I'll leave it as I want to borrow their strimmer later on.

Breakfast. I need to lower my cholesterol, but what is the point of being able to have the time for a leisurely wrinkly breakfast and then just have a piece of crispbread with low fat spread.

Sod it, I'll have a fry up again.

Things You Can Safely Put Off Until Tomorrow

One of the joys of being a wrinkly is having that little bit of extra time on your hands. You might be retired, you are probably not putting quite so much effort into trying to meet members of the opposite sex, and unlike younger people, you may not find it quite so necessary to be constantly phoning, texting, emailing, and updating your social networking websites.

But somehow, you're quite busy. What you need is WTM or Wrinkly Time Management.

This means deferring the not so pressing tasks, commitments and other flipping nuisances that clutter up your day.

The diet

George Orwell said, 'At 50, everyone has the face he deserves.' He could have added, 'and the body too.' Let's face it, if you've gone this long without adhering to a diet it's hardly worth bothering now is it?

Saving for a rainy day

The rainy day, my friend, is already here in the form of wrinkliehood. Spend it while you can!

Tidying the loft

The loft is the upstairs equivalent of under the carpet, but on a bigger scale. Instead of hiding bits of fluff and so on, it is the convenient receptacle for all the things that might 'come in useful one day'. Which may in theory be true, but only if you could remember what the hell was up there in the first place. It can wait.

Trying to find out what's in fashion

Without naming names, we all know the kind of shops wrinklies like to buy their clothes from. Reliable, trusted chains that don't have any truck with 'cutting edge' fashion.

But that doesn't mean to say the wrinkly wants to look like either Darby or Joan just yet. Shopping at High Street, Middle England means wrinklies don't have to think about fashion at all. They can be suited and booted in safe, vaguely contemporary attire without consulting Vogue. Perhaps we need our own fashion magazine called Fogue?

Cleaning the house

What was it Quentin Crisp said? Something about not bothering to dust because after six months it doesn't get any dustier? He's got a point. Plus of course, you can't build up your bodily resistance if you're living in a clinically clean environment can you? Well, that's our excuse anyway.

Mowing the lawn

Do you think Adam possessed a lawn mower in the Garden of Eden? Precisely. It's unnatural. It would also be interesting to see if Mr Crisp's dictum held true for grass too? After a certain time does the grass simply not get any higher? It's probably all academic anyway, as after a while you'd never be able to find the lawn mower out there.

Learning another language

You've lasted this long with *deux bierres s'il vous plaît*, so why bother?

Things You Should Have Done Today But Didn't

But enough of these trifling things that you will defer to another day. What about those really important things that you should have done but never quite got around to?

Written that novel

Well at least, starting it. You read somewhere that everyone has a novel in them. If only you could come up with perhaps a title or even an idea for a title. But no, as the sun sinks down again over that unmown lawn the unwritten novel stays unwritten.

Eaten your five a day

You know it makes sense, you know it's good for you and you really should have but you haven't quite done it again have you? But surely the currants in your garibaldis count, and the leaves in your tea, and the lemon in your gin and tonic, and the grapes in your wine...

Done your exercise

You know it's important after a certain age to keep your body in trim, and you've still got that magazine article you cut out about gentle exercise for the over 50s, but you haven't quite got round to it yet have you? Yes, we know that in your humble opinion it isn't gentle enough, but walking from the TV to the fridge simply isn't enough exercise – even if you do do it 20 times a day.

Recycled

You put your rubbish in the proper bins on rubbish day, but the rest of the time you're about as green as a radish.

Yes, you have good intentions, but life's too short to wash your baked bean tins isn't it?

Learned how to text

Your children virtually forced you to buy a mobile phone, and that, as far as you were concerned, is about as modern and up to date as you were prepared to get. Then you started to get texts from your grandchildren saying things like 'thnx 4 mi xmas prezzie' and you're expected to text back.

What's the point of being a wrinkly if you're going to act like a 12 year-old?

Fitted your panic alarm

Another of your kids' bright ideas, and still sitting in the box it came in.

Checked your blood pressure, cholesterol, etc

There comes a point in a wrinkly's life when you feel like a car that's having a daily MOT test.

Most old bangers manage to chunter on quite nicely without them most of the time – and cars do too.

Invited the neighbours in for a drink

You keep meaning to, but by the time you've had breakfast, then elevenses, and lunch, it's time for a little nap, then Countdown, then it's dinner, and 40 winks in front of the box, and blow us down, it's bedtime again! Where does the time go?

Counting Your Wrinkly Blessings

It's so easy to look on the downside of wrinklyhood isn't it?

Well, to be fair, there are one or two things you might not be over the moon about, but let's not dwell on those; let's look at the upside.

You're not dead

Being dead does have its advantages of course: no more tax, no more aches and pains, and no more ear-bashings from your wrinkly other half.

But it's not ideal by any means. So, you're a bit older than you used to be but so is everyone else, and you're still here to tell the tale.

You're not young

Youth is overrated. Would you really want to spend all your waking hours either texting people or reading texts, or worrying about who hasn't texted you?

Would you want to be self-confined to the house for a fortnight because you had a tiny little spot on your nose? Would you really want to try to walk with your trouser waist perched just above your knees because it's fashionable?

You possess wisdom

Yes, young people like to think they know it all, and they may have a slight advantage when it comes to fixing your crashed computer, but do they know which cutlery to use first at a wedding reception? Do they know how to spell any word of more than one syllable (or sometimes just one syllable)?

Do they remember what the government before last was like and know not to vote for them? Can a Kentucky fried chicken fly?

You have fewer worries

With a bit of luck your mortgage is a dim and distant memory. You may even be in profit if you're charging your teenage and adult children rent!

You don't care what you look like. Well, up to a point. Even wrinklies have some pride. But you're not a slave to fashion, and you won't be devastated if the postman catches you in your jim jams (some hope with the modern postal system!)

You are at the end of your working life

Even if you're still working, the end is in sight! No more clocking on, bunking off, trying to invent new excuses for throwing a sickie, having to go to leaving parties of people you don't even like, contributing to collections every time someone gets married, has a baby (not necessarily in that order) or runs a half marathon. Freedom!

You don't care any more

'Beyond dignity' might be putting it a bit strong, but frankly, who cares if anyone laughs at your dress sense, talks behind your back, questions your sexuality, calls you a racist, flashes a V sign because of some minor motoring misdemeanour or other such trivialities.

Mind you, if they said your garden looked a bit on the untidy side you would of course be well within your rights to give them a sock on the jaw.

How To Look Good Wrinkly

These days there is absolutely no shortage of role models for the wrinkly gorgeousness aspirant. Did we mention somewhere else in this book such names as Joan Collins, Sophia Loren, Helen Mirren, Raquel Welch, Jane Fonda, Sean Connery, Harrison Ford, Clint Eastwood...?
So, what's their secret?

No artificial help

Never mind the Botox. What's the point of being, ahem, of a certain age, if you look like a box-fresh Barbie doll? Actors everywhere adhere to that dramatic dictum: 'you can't emote with a face full of 'Bote."

Besides, people will be highly suspicious of an actor playing say, Moses, if he looks about 12.

A few million dollars

Yes, regular, unlimited access to fabulous food, designer clothes, expensive gyms and tanning salons can help – so keep filling in those lottery tickets!

Great lighting

Actors have the advantage of being able to dish out official photos, taken in subdued lighting with perhaps a Vaseline smeared soft-focus lens. Then there may be a bit of jiggery pokery with some clever photographic software to enhance those lined, and frankly southbound, features.

So for us non-thespian wrinklies that probably means having a life-size professional photo taken, and then wearing it like a mask at all times.

False Memory Syndrome

Somehow we have a fixed idea in our minds of actors at their peak regardless of how old they've got, or even look. In our mind's eye they are still just as they were when we first set our caps at them. Perhaps this is why Mickey Mouse never looks any older, despite being the wrong side of 80. But actors, and famous rodents aside, what else can the wrinkly do to keep the years at bay?

Bare flesh

It's all right for the doctor to see you in the buff. He's probably bound by a Hippocratic oath or something not to breathe a word about what's baggy, saggy or wrinkly about your body, on pain of being struck off.

Not so your friends. Keep your wrinkles under wraps.

Fancy dress parties

If you restrict your socialising purely to fancy dress parties then you will be able to cover up the worst of what the years have done to you. This might explain why certain ageing fashion designers always appear to be in fancy dress.

Good works

Have you noticed how many retired people start doing good works – helping out at charity shops, taking old people out for the day, that sort of thing? There is of course a philanthropic element to all this, but it has the marvellous side benefit of making the helper look younger in contrast to the helpees.

Who wouldn't look quite perky next to a nonagenarian?

What You Intend, And What You Actually Do

We wrinklies like our resolutions. What we don't like so much is actually sticking to them. For example:

Intention: I'm not going to end up like my father/mother.
Actuality: You get mistaken for them by even older, and perhaps slightly confused members of the family.

Intention: I'm not going to become a grumpy old man/woman.
Actuality: Your tongue is feared and dreaded more widely than that of a venomous snake.

Intention: I'm going to keep myself fit.
Actuality: If you moved any less in an average day you would probably be dusted by anyone cleaning the room.

Intention: I'll try to keep up with all this modern technology.
Actuality: You thought broadband was a type of margarine.

Intention: I'd like to do a bit of travelling.
Actuality: It's all such a hassle. Even preparations for a trip to the supermarket stop just short of injections, passports, and travel pills.

Intention: I'm not going to get stuck in a rut.
Actuality: You're still watching the same TV programmes that you did 30 years ago, but now it's on oldies TV channels and DVD.

Intention: I'll try to keep up with the latest clothes fashions.
Actuality: They don't seem to do the latest fashions in a 44-inch waist.

Intention: I'll start doing something useful for the local community now I've got a bit more time on my hands.
Actuality: I'm writing more letters to the local paper about dog mess, fly tipping, and the outrageous council tax rises.

Intention: I'll try not to have the first drink of the day before the sun's over the yard arm.
Actuality: The sun is over the yard arm somewhere in the world by 11am isn't it?

Intention: I'll try to keep up with younger bands and their music.
Actuality: Tribute bands are usually quite young aren't they?

Intention: I'll research my entire family tree now I've got the time.
Actuality: How do you get this computer going again?

How To Live Cheaply

Wrinklies can often find themselves a bit short of cash what with retirement, redundancy, and possibly several other words beginning with 're'.

It is therefore essential that wrinklies have a few tricks and tips up their cardie sleeves to eke out those sparse coppers in their later years.

It is rather a shock to the system when your spending goes from huge to Scrooge, but as always, the wrinkly will bear it all with characteristic fortitude, forbearance and dignity.

Eating the cat's food

When you look at the labels on cat food these days you start to think 'wait a minute, this animal's eating better than I am!' Tenderloin of beef, trout with mixed vegetables, ocean fish, chicken breasts with vegetables and brown rice. What's going on here?!

Now we're not suggesting of course that you open a tin of cat food and consume the contents yourself, tempting though this may be. No, you cook yourself the tenderloin of beef, trout or whatever and let the cat have the leftovers. The money you save on not buying this ridiculous cat food will enable you to eat like a king.

Turn off the heating

Even with your wrinkly winter fuel allowance it still costs an arm, a leg, and probably several other parts of your anatomy to heat the house during the cold weather.

The trick is to arrange with your wrinkly friends that they will all come to your house on, say, Monday, then you turn off the heating for the rest of the week while you go to another wrinkly's house on Tuesday, then a different one's on Wednesday and so on.

You will cut your heating bill by 85%, you will be having a house party every day of the week, and you may even be in profit from your Winter fuel allowance. Fantastic!

Run your own postal service

With the price of a first class stamp now approaching the equivalent of the national debt of a small African country it is time for wrinklies everywhere to unite.

What with sending postal orders and presents to grandchildren, writing letters of complaint to various companies, and of course your ongoing correspondence to newspapers national and local, your postal bills are now quite sizeable. But help is at hand!

Wrinklies all over the country have free local travel. It should not therefore be beyond the wit of man for wrinklies to form a national network that passes mail on from one wrinkly's local area to another.

Before long the entire country would be one vast postal system with letters and parcels passing from hand to wrinkled hand.

It should be possible to get a letter from Land's End to John O'Groats in less than a week which may actually be quicker than the current second class 'service'.

Wrinklies of the world unite! You have nothing to lose but your chain letters!

New Year Resolutions You Might Keep

Just after your two weeks of gluttony and over-consumption, otherwise known as Christmas, you will probably start thinking about how you will reinvent yourself in the New Year so you become a better wrinkly and generally all round wonderful human being.

To make things easier for yourself and so you don't fall short of your high expectations you should only make New Year resolutions that you have a hope in hell of keeping. For example:

Slowing down a bit

Taking the law of unintended consequences to its logical conclusion, you will slow down whether you want to or not. As long as you don't actually grind to a complete standstill it's nothing to worry about.

Giving up something

People always make the mistake of resolving to give up something they enjoy. What's the point of that? It's so much easier to give up something you don't enjoy, e.g. eating offal, or cleaning out the cat litter, or being polite to double-glazing salesmen on the doorstep.

Not running the marathon

It's all very well to get into the record books for being the oldest person to run the marathon, or the fastest pensioner, but you don't want to be in there for the wrong reasons, e.g. the shortest distance ever covered before collapsing in a heap.

New Year Resolutions You Probably Won't Keep

Oh, if you really must. Go on, make a fool of yourself. Make a great long list of all the wonderful things you're going to do come January 1st; all the things you're going to give up; all the ways you're going to be a model citizen, a paragon of virtue and all that other stuff. But don't come crying to us when it all goes pear-shaped, or more likely when you go all pear-shaped after your diet comes to a sticky (and probably sweet) end on January 2nd.

Here are the ones you probably won't keep (though congrats all round if you do):

The diet

If you've been resolving to lose weight every year since about 1971 and failed what hope do you think you've got now? And why should you care anyway? If you were meant to lose weight why did they invent expandable waist trousers?

Smoking

Ditto smoking. If you were going to give it up you would have done so by now. And if you're prepared to shell out the six quid a packet or whatever it costs these days you must be pretty determined to carry on puffing.

Cutting down on drinking

Considering you've probably never accurately evaluated your weekly alcohol consumption it's going to be quite difficult to determine whether you've actually reduced your intake. Which is probably exactly what you'll argue next time someone 'twists your arm' to have just one more.

Chapter 11:
Life, The Wrinklyverse and Everything

When lying in their beds at night, wrinklies will often contemplate the meaning of life. Well, first they might contemplate the gas bill they received that morning and where to go for their holidays this year. Nevertheless eventually they will get onto the great questions of existence.

What is the meaning and purpose of life? What answers can science provide us? Are there great secrets which are deliberately being withheld from us by the government?

What's it all about?

Wrinklies are very concerned by these big questions. For a start they can't believe they have lived as long as they have and still not managed to crack them.

Failing that couldn't they have found a way of cheating to get hold of the answer? Couldn't someone have surreptitiously slipped the solution to them by now or at least given them details of a website where you could look it up?

Unfortunately if a wrinkly ever knew the meaning of life, it now seems to have slipped their wrinkly old memory. Wrinklies are thus left sitting in the exam hall of life feeling as though they have done insufficient revision to pass. Nevertheless others will inevitably regard wrinklies as sources of great wisdom.

By their time of life wrinklies should resemble great gurus or venerable ancient philosophers. They should all wear great flowing gowns. They should have enormous grey beards and big bulging bald heads. Possibly male wrinklies should have these as well.

All wrinklies should look like solemn thinkers cogitating on the deepest insights of which man is capable.

This is not however what wrinklies usually look like. Wrinkly men are often balding and pot bellied and dressed in flat caps and beige zip up jackets. Wrinkly ladies often have curly permed hair and dress in comfortable slacks and nice cardies. Neither of these images tend to spring to mind when people hear the phrase 'great philosopher' but perhaps they should.

Because of their age and experience, wrinklies rightly believe that they should be regarded and valued as elders of their community. Many people do regard and value wrinklies as elders. This is why they refer to them by names such as 'Grandad', 'Grandma' or 'You old dear'.

Nevertheless the fact that they either don't know or have forgotten the answers to life's great questions remains a source of potential embarrassment for wrinklies.

Wrinklies fear young people will come to them demanding to know what the meaning of life is and they will only be able to respond with statements such as 'Always remember to wear sensible shoes' and 'A little of what you fancy does you good.'

So when put on the spot what can wrinklies say or do to make themselves look a bit wiser and more inscrutable?

Indeed could the secrets of being a wrinkly be a key to the secrets of life itself? Perhaps we are all living not in a universe but in a wrinklyverse!

How To Look Like A Wise Old Wrinkly Who Might Possibly Know The Meaning Of Life

Do: sit puffing slowly on an old Meerschaum pipe in order to cultivate the air of an ageing academic.
Don't: sit blowing bubbles from a brightly coloured plastic pipe in order to cultivate the air of a complete idiot.

Do: wander around in a long flowing gown like an ancient philosopher.
Don't: wander around in a long flowing gown open to reveal your backside like a patient who has escaped from a secure unit.

Do: give carefully considered answers to those who come to you with life's great questions.
Don't: wander up and down the high street shouting at anyone who passes by.

Do: sit cross-legged surrounded by your disciples.
Don't: sit cross-legged surrounded by your disciples while repeatedly raising your left buttock to break wind.

Do: sit slowly stroking your chin while contemplating life's mysteries.
Don't: sit slowly scratching your groin while contemplating the fungal infection you have recently developed.

Do: sit dispensing words of wisdom.
Don't: sit dispensing the words of Norman Wisdom.

Wrinkly Conspiracy Theories

The Moon landings were faked by wrinkly actors in a film studio: that's why the astronauts appear to move so slowly and clumsily on the Moon surface. One of the astronauts even resorted to playing golf on the Moon thereby clearly revealing himself to be a wrinkly.

A UFO landed at Roswell, New Mexico in 1947; pictures of the autopsy performed on the Roswell alien show an odd looking bald figure with a protuberant veined skull. Clearly the Roswell alien was a wrinkly from another galaxy who had come to make contact with wrinklies on Earth. The story therefore had to be hushed up by young people.

Elvis Presley faked his own death: Elvis 'died' aged 42 years old. Exactly the time when he would have been turning wrinkly! Obviously it was all a hoax to stop him wiggling his pelvis before he put an artificial hip out.

The world is governed by a secret all-powerful organisation: well, they certainly never tell us wrinklies what's going on.

Shakespeare didn't write the plays commonly ascribed to him: this is a conspiracy theory put about by young people who cannot believe that a wrinkly slaphead like Shakespeare could have written his plays and that they must therefore have been written by someone younger with a full head of hair like Christopher Marlowe.

Global warming is a hoax: this is a tall tale clearly perpetrated by the government in an effort to cut winter fuel payments to older wrinklies.

Feng Shui For Wrinklies

Feng Shui is the wise and ancient Chinese art of where to put stuff. Wrinklies are also wise and ancient and spend much of their time wondering where to put all the rubbish they have accumulated during their lives. So which of the essential principles of Feng Shui specifically apply to wrinklies?

Avoid placing a mirror opposite your front door

This is good advice for wrinklies because otherwise every time they walk through their front door they will be terrified by the sight of the shrivelled old person standing opposite them and this may cause them to drop their shopping.

Hallways should be bright places

Your front door should open into a bright well-lit hallway because otherwise wrinklies' photochromatic varifocals can be slow to react causing them to immediately be plunged into darkness and fall over.

Beware of straight roads leading to your front door

The front of your house should not face a straight road. Wrinklies should pay particular heed to this advice especially if the brakes on their wrinkly old cars need attention or their reactions are a little slow. Otherwise the Ford Focus will end up parked for the night in the living room... again.

Positioning your bedroom at the end of a long corridor is unlucky

This is because wrinkly house guests may wander in during the middle of the night thinking they have found your bathroom and you will then wake up the next morning feeling slightly damp.

Wind chimes around your garden will make you popular

Or maybe they'll just make so much racket you won't hear the neighbours shouting at you to take them down.

Exposed overhead beams are sources of bad energy

Or more to the point they are sources of dirty great bruises on your wrinkly bonce. To diffuse the bad energy, hang a wind chime from the beam. The irritating tinkling sound will then alert you to the fact that you have just bashed your head on the beam as well as helping to drown out the shouting and swearing that follows a moment later.

Don't hang mirrors in the bedroom

Otherwise they will keep shattering every time you get undressed in front of them. And that's just from the sound of the high pitched screaming that usually follows.

The ratio of windows to doors in a room should not exceed 3:1

Otherwise there is a corresponding 3:1 chance that a forgetful wrinkly will attempt to leave the room via one of the windows. This advice is particularly important for wrinklies living in high rise flats. One door and one window per room at least gives you a 50/50 chance of survival every time you pop out to put the kettle on.

Keep the toilet door closed

Particularly while you're in there and you have guests in the house.

Wrinklies' Universal Scientific Laws

The following are the fundamental scientific laws
underlying the wrinkly universe:

- For every action there is an equal and opposite pain in
  your knee joints.
- A body will remain in a state of rest or at least it will
  until its wrinkly bed partner tells it to get up and
  make a cup of tea.
- The speed of light in a vacuum is constant but the
  speed of your vacuum depends on the depth of your
  shag pile.
- The energy in a closed system remains constant unless
  it's just got back from the shops when it will feel a bit
  tired.
- Every particle in the universe attracts every other
  particle but the older wrinklier particles tend to get
  less of a look in.
- The likelihood of bumping into someone you know
  when you go out is inversely proportional to how
  much you want to see them.
- The speed at which people move away from you in
  the high street is in direct proportion to whether they
  think you noticed them or not.
- Computers will keep on getting smarter but they will
  never get so smart that they won't mess up your direct
  debit payments.
- If you let Archimedes use your bath, you'll end up
  with water all over your bathroom floor.

- A watched kettle never boils (Boil's Law).
- Simon Cowell earns more money than you do (Susan Boyle's Law).
- Your sleeve will always catch on the door handle (Hook's Law).
- Things are more difficult than they should be (More's Law).
- Grated carrot and cabbage in mayonnaise goes nicely with a salad (Coles Law).
- If an apple drops out of a tree onto your head you'll run round in agony for several minutes (Newton's Law of Motion).
- I'm not certain where I left my keys (Heisenberg's Uncertainty Principle).
- Your lottery numbers will win the jackpot the week you don't buy a ticket.
- If you are looking for an item in the supermarket, someone will appear and stand in front of it at the precise moment you finally locate it.
- Mechanical and electrical appliances will break down the day after the guarantee runs out.
- If you are looking for an item in the supermarket and finally give up and ask an assistant, you will then discover that you are in fact standing right next to it thereby making yourself look like a complete idiot.

The Wrinkly Universe

If you're ever feeling a bit old, just think how the universe itself must feel. The universe is currently about 13.5 billion years old (and probably by the time you read this, it will be slightly older). The universe is therefore only slightly less old than you feel. No wonder it's in the state it's in. Not only that but no-one ever remembers its birthday.

The universe is therefore the ultimate wrinkly. Like other wrinklies the universe doesn't seem to be doing quite as much as it did in its earlier days, it seems to be moving slower than it used to, it's feeling colder, it's looking more dishevelled and it's a very very long time since it enjoyed a Big Bang.

Also like other wrinklies not only is the universe extremely old, it has been steadily increasing in size since the year dot. So if you ever feel depressed about putting on weight, just think of the universe.

When it began, the universe was about the size of an atom and now look at it! Even with the most stringent diet, the universe is clearly going to have some considerable difficulty getting back to its original size!

Many wonder whether, like its fellow wrinklies, the universe still has any particular purpose any more. Some fear the day is approaching when the universe will finally collapse.

Nevertheless, like many other wrinklies, the universe seems to carry on regardless with its regular routine day after day.

The planets in our solar system are around 4.5 billion years old. Yes, we know you remember the day some of the newer ones formed.

At 4.5 billion years old the planets are clearly a bit wrinkly. Nevertheless the universe must see them as young upstarts and thus regard them with suspicion. Planets however even look wrinkly being covered in craters and having dry, cracked surfaces. Planets are surely crying out for a bit of Oil of Olay.

And to further prove planets are wrinklies: they are often grey-looking; they spend their days wandering round in a circle while being battered with all that the universe can throw at them; they fear falling into black holes; and many of them are shrouded by atmospheres in which a lot of people would find it difficult to breathe.

Yes, the planets might as well all go round the sun on planet-sized Zimmer frames!

It is therefore clearly a wrinkly universe.

In fact when you think about it, the entire future is wrinkly.

By the time the future arrives today's young people will be old. Also thanks to advances in medical science there will be an ever increasing number of wrinklies around.

The inevitable fate of the universe is therefore not that it will be full of glamorous young astronauts zipping around the galaxies but that it will gradually fill up with wrinklies.

Those may not be stars twinkling in the sky but the grey heads of an infinite number of wrinklies!

Frequently Asked Questions About Life On Other Planets

Is there life on other planets and if so why can't we see it?

We never see any signs of life when we look at other planets in the universe. This is because we are only able to use telescopes to look at other planets at night-time when it is dark. Clearly at night-time wrinklies have all gone to bed or are sitting in the back room watching television. The reason we have not detected life on other planets is therefore because all extra-terrestrial beings must be wrinklies.

What do aliens look like?

Large balding heads with protuberant veins. Withered looking limbs. They're wrinklies! (see Wrinkly Conspiracy Theories p.155)

Why are UFO sightings only ever reported in remote areas where few people live?

Remote locations with few people around are exactly the sorts of places a wrinkly might go for a short break or day out. UFOs that visit Earth must therefore be piloted by alien wrinklies. We can thus deduce that the insides of UFOs must have a tartan rug on the backseat and a little nodding dog and a box of tissues on the parcel shelf at the back.

Why does it seem that messages we have sent out into space have not been picked up by alien civilisations?

Because it's all wrinklies out there. They're all a bit deaf. They probably didn't hear any of our messages.

Why have alien civilisations not made more attempt to contact us?

That's wrinklies for you. They like to keep themselves to themselves.

Are alien civilisations greatly more advanced than our own?

Alien civilisations are vastly more scientifically and technically advanced than us. Unfortunately the wrinklies who live in these alien civilisations have probably never been able to take advantage of the scientific and technical advances available to them. This is because the instruction books that came with all their advanced scientific and technical technology had a lot of small print and were a bit complicated to read. This is another reason why we don't receive regular communications or visits from alien wrinklies.

Why would aliens come to our planet?

If they're wrinklies, mainly for medical treatment on the NHS or to visit National Trust properties.

How long would aliens take to travel to Earth?

If they travelled from Proxima Centauri, the nearest star to us after the sun, their journey would take 76,000 years. So even if they weren't wrinkly when they set off, they certainly would be by the time they got here. It is possible aliens may have more advanced spaceship technology. This will not however speed up their journeys because, being wrinklies, they will need frequent toilet stops and get a bit lost travelling round unfamiliar solar systems. Also, being wrinklies, they might just decide to leave the spaceship at home and come here by bus instead.

Wise Utterances For Philosophical Wrinklies

- Life is what you make it. Your excuse can therefore be that no-one ever gave you a proper set of assembly instructions.
- Life is a sexually transmitted disease. And you weren't even the one who got the sex.
- Life is a lottery so look on the bright side. Even getting the booby prize is fun!
- Life is like a box of chocolates. When you get to a certain age, there's less to choose from, they're all coffee creams and the ones you've had up to now have rotted your teeth.
- Life is a series of things going wrong and the biggest thing going wrong happens right at the end.
- Life is like having a ticket to the greatest show on Earth but you'll probably spend all your time trying to find somewhere to park.
- No-one can tell you the precise meaning of life although many will try and palm you off with a misleading translation.
- Not only is life not fair, there isn't even a complaints desk.
- Life is the sum of all your choices. This may cause you to ask how can I have been wrong that often?
- Life is like an annoying neighbour with a big car. It goes past far too quickly and invariably fails to acknowledge you.
- Live your life as though each day is your last although this will mean that friends and family will become increasingly annoyed to see you again each morning.

The Wrinkly Whisperer

You've heard of amazing animal experts such as the horse whisperer, the dog whisperer, the cat whisperer and the slightly less successful three-toed sloth whisperer.

These people seem to have an extraordinary ability to understand what animals are trying to tell them although this is usually along the lines of, 'Could you speak up? I can't hear what you're saying because you keep whispering!'

Wrinklies also have a great affinity with other species (with the notable exception of young people that is). But what would different animals say to a wrinkly?

Animal	What They Would Say To A Wrinkly
Cat	I am your master and you will feed me, look after me, clean up after me and do everything I command from this day forward!
Budgie	And that goes for me too!
Dog	I've noticed that when we're out for a walk, you seem to need a wee about as often as I do.
Goldfish	So tell me, what's it like living with such a poor short-term memory?
Tortoise	Is that really the fastest you can go?
Snail	Don't worry. I'll go on ahead and tell the tortoise to wait.
Lion	It's OK I'm not going to eat you. Not when you're clearly so far past your 'Best before' date.
Skunk	Can you smell something funny in here?
Cow	Blimey! I thought mine hung a bit low!
Elephant	Blimey! You're more grey and wrinkly than I am!
Cat (again)	So are you getting me my dinner or what?

Chapter 12:
Tomorrow's World

When you're a wrinkly today increasingly seems like
tomorrow. Every day seems to bring some bewildering
change, technological or otherwise, that seems bizarre,
baffling, or just plain daft.

Once upon a time, not so long ago, you had things
called records, that you played on record players. These
had been around since you were a tot, and probably since
your parents were tots too.

OK, your mum and dad probably had to get used to
the vast cultural shift of 78 rpm records being jettisoned
in favour of those little 45s, and having to plug the record
player into the wall rather than using one of things like a
starting handle (note to younger readers: that was what
you used to start your car with back in the day when
Churchill was a politician and not a talking dog).

But essentially, a record was a record regardless of what
speed it revolved at!

Then came cassettes and CDs, and yes, CDs were sort
of like mini records that came in miniaturised cases that
mimicked ye olde album covers.

Now they're going too. To be replaced by what?

Nothing! Nothing, you ask? Now you have to
'download' your favourite tunes via a computer (what
if you don't have a computer?) and put it on your iPod,
whatever that may be. It sound like an awful lot of faffing

about, and you don't even get a record cover to hold in your grubby mitts.

And they charge you for this. Ee, it's like buying thin air as your granny might have said.

Now they're talking about digital TV, and how we'll all have to change our TV sets – and our radios too.

Isn't it strange, that while TV is still broadcasting *Coronation Street*, and radio still has *The Archers* and *Desert Island Discs* and the shipping forecast and all those other shows from the mists of time we suddenly need all this new-fangled equipment to watch or listen to them on?

And don't even get us started on videos. What a boon it was when they invented the video and you could record *Eastenders* while you were at the bingo or in the pub.

Then some bright spark decided it was too simple, too convenient, and we'd need DVDs instead. Only problem was, you couldn't record on them to begin with.

Then they brought in something called blu-ray. What's that when it's at home? Is it related to bluetooth? And what's HDTV? Why do they have to keep changing things? Progress, they say.

But no, we wrinklies have been around long enough to know that all this talk of progress and technological advancement is just moonshine.

Tomorrow's world will be just like today's world but they'll just have more scientific excuses when it all goes pear-shaped.

Inventions Wrinklies Are Waiting For

"Build a better mousetrap and the world will beat a path to your door" is what Ralph Waldo Emerson has often been credited with saying.

These days it would probably be: "Build a better mousetrap and you might not get the mickey taken out of you on *Dragon's Den.*"

What we really need though is a sort of *Dragon's Den* for wrinklies. If such a programme existed this is what we'd like to see on it:

Large print road signs

You know what it's like, you're driving along and you see one of those road signs with a big exclamation mark warning of some terrible hazard, but the writing underneath is minuscule. Well, minuscule for the average wrinkly anyway. And if that means giant road signs with other road signs warning you to look out for them so be it.

Pill-dispensing cuckoo clocks

Frankly it's a faff. You have to remember to take your little blue pill at breakfast time, your little pink pill at half past eleven, two yellow pills at 3.30pm, a white pill with your evening meal and your disgusting brown ones just before bed. If you're taking even one of those pills to help your memory then you're on a loser from the start. What you need is a clock, a bit like a cuckoo clock, but instead of a wooden cuckoo popping out you get a little man in a white coat carrying your pill du heure. What could be simpler?

Walk-in cars

It's all very well getting in and out of cars if you're a sprightly young thing but when your age is fast heading towards the national speed limit and your joints are in more need of oiling than your car then it's not such a piece of cake. They invented a walk-in bath for people who don't bend in the right places, why not a walk-in car too? There's a fortune to be made by some lucky person.

Proper sized telephones

Some of these phones nowadays aren't much bigger than a Mars bar. By the time you've picked them up and fiddled around trying to find which button to press, the caller has rung off.

An exploding handbag

Old ladies with handbags full of pension money are seen as easy targets by some criminal elements. This bag would explode within ten seconds of being snatched by a simple 'tug reaction' mechanism. They might have to work on how to avoid your pension money being blown to bits as well though...

Ride-on supermarket trolleys

At a certain time of life we don't want to be pushing trolleys full of HobNobs and cat food around the supermarket. What we need are ride-on trolleys. They would have to be for the exclusive use of wrinklies though; you wouldn't want boy racers with trolleys full of cheap lager cutting you up on the corners. The other advantage is that people would no longer be able to accuse you of being off your trolley.

The Wrinklies' Guide To The Modern World

Who was it who said the past was a foreign country? Well, they obviously hadn't seen the future, or what is now known as the present.

We wrinklies were brought up on Dan Dare and other space exploring heroes. We were led to believe that by the 21st century we would all be walking around skyscrapered streets in space suits, flying down to the shops using our jet-packs and having pet robots doing all our chores for us. Ha! Tosh and nonsense!

The nearest we get to a space suit is a shell suit and the prospect of getting a stairlift is hardly an adequate replacement for our long promised jet packs.

Surely we're due some sort of compensation for the future we were promised but never got. Instead we've got a future nobody expected!

What nobody imagined was people of a certain age – all right, wrinklies – walking around in jeans, T-shirts and trainers like superannuated James Deans. We had no idea that the morning post would be delivered in the afternoon or that our fifteen minutes of fame would be on CCTV.

Oh it's a rum place all right, this modern world. For example:

Coffee

Well for a start there's no such thing as 'a coffee' any more. It's a latte, or a cappuccino, or an Americano, or a Mocha or some such daft thing. Whatever it is, it certainly isn't our cup of tea.

And you can't get a small one, it has to be 'regular' (dreadful Americanism meaning large) or large (meaning huge) or possibly grande (meaning it's served in a bucket and will keep you in the toilet for the rest of the day). Then they serve this concoction in a cardboard cup and ask you to stump up almost half a week's pension for the privilege!

Friendship

Once upon a time you met people and they became your friends – or not, as the case may be. Now you have to have friends on social networking websites. People you've not met. People you're never likely to meet. But they're your 'friends'. If you can't invite them round for tea they can't be proper friends can they?

Technology

What's a Blackberry for example? You hear of people who can't live without their Blackberries. Maybe it's some sort of pacemaker or dialysis machine?

Twitter. For the birds. Well it sounds like budgie food. Skype. Something like Sky Plus maybe? The problem is that when you reach wrinklyhood you're constantly bombarded with all this new technology day in, day out.

Hardly a day passes without some new bit of kit coming onto the market that we all 'must have'. How long before we're all expected to walk around with a Hadron collider in our pocket? iPad – it sounds like something the doctor would give you to put over your peepers after your cataract operation.

Other annoying things

And what's this new fashion for giving everyone daft nicknames? Jennifer Lopez became J-Lo, Boris Johnson became BoJo, and Susan Boyle became SuBo. Does this mean that if your name is Susan Moore you have to be SuMo or that if you were unluckily christened Boris Zonk, you're going to be BoZo?

So-called entertainment

Have you watched *Question Time* lately? Unfortunately it's no longer a simple case of watching it; you can 'push the red button' if you're watching digitally, follow it on Twitter, email in your comments, phone, or even write in using ye olde postal system. If you miss it you can watch on the iPlayer whatever that may be.

In the old days, if you missed a programme you missed it. 'End of!' (as soap opera characters annoyingly tend to say these days). Radio programmes are available as 'podcasts' which sounds like some unpleasant plaster of Paris support around your nether regions. It's impossible to miss anything! Even if you really don't want to watch it!

Even more technology!

Nothing's simple anymore is it? Whenever you phone anyone it's a rare treat if you actually get through to a human being straight away.

More likely it's the answerphone or voicemail, or a multichoice switchboard. Press one for this, and two for that and three to top yourself. Then when the call finally goes through to someone with a welcome ringing tone it suddenly cuts to piped music.

Is this what happened to all those robots we were promised? They don't do your housework for you but you do get to speak to them whenever you phone any large institution. For ten minutes, an android will boss you around telling you which button on your telephone keypad to press next. Weren't they supposed to obey us?

Has anyone ever calculated the number of man hours wasted every year listening to this garbage? It would probably be enough to rebuild Hadrian's Wall, put up the third terminal at Heathrow, and solve the meaning of life – with enough time left over to work out whether the title of *Britain's Got Talent* is a statement or a question.

Yes, the modern world is a strange land indeed, and the wrinkly is like a time traveller variously marvelling at and being repulsed by it all.

The great advantage for the wrinkly though is he or she can mentally travel back in time to 'the good old days' when the post was delivered three times a day, when the only person wearing a hoodie was Father Christmas, when tweets were the dawn chorus, and when a financial crisis was the pound being worth less than four dollars.

If you told the kids of today how marvellous life was in your wrinkle-free youth they wouldn't believe you. Not that they'd hear you anyway; they'd have some electrical device plugged into their ears and by the time they'd got it out you'd have forgotten what you were saying.

The Ideal Things For Wrinklies To Wake Up To

Probably the best thing to wake up to would be not being a wrinkly, but hey, you can't have everything, and if you did, as comedian Steven Wright once noted, where would you keep it anyway?

Wrinklies enjoy their little luxuries. After a lifetime of work and bringing up kids, not for them the lights and the sights, but a bit of gentle relaxation. For example:

A bit of peace and quiet

As soon as you wake up you hear the rumble of traffic, the clatter of milk bottles and the paperboy's squeaky bike. As the day goes on there's more and more unwanted noise. Older people aren't actually hard of hearing, they voluntarily go a bit Mutt 'n' Jeff to avoid all the racket.

Not 5.00am

Why is that when you get older you need less sleep? If you're retired it's sometimes hard enough to fill the day with useful things to do even if you wake up at nine o'clock.

Tea in bed

Why can't they extend the Meal on Wheels service to tea in bed? They could call it Char by Car. OK, it would probably mean a bit more on your council tax but ooh, wouldn't it be lovely?

A time lapse

If it can happen on the TV series *Life on Mars*, why not in real life? Just as long as you don't end up in the 70s or 80s. The Swinging Sixties might be nice, or those reliable old black & white 50s (after rationing finished of course). Just imagine waking up and looking out of the window and not seeing a car in sight, or a bollard, or a yellow line... bliss.

A gorgeous other half

Millionaires do it every day. Even if they're ninety years old. As long as they've got enough noughts on their bank statement they seem to have beautiful young members of the opposite sex swarming round them. Noughty but nice.

To find that it's all been a dream

Yes, you've just had this horrific dream that you're past your prime, you've got more lines than BT, your body's stiff in all the wrong places and your entire life savings might not even be quite enough for a new set of garden furniture. Then you wake up to find you're a 23 year old millionaire snoozing on your yacht in the Mediterranean.

Proper music on the radio

Music with tunes, singers who can actually sing – it's not much to ask is it? It comes to a pretty pass when even Radio 2 is playing some dreadful racket with people shouting and swearing and Reith knows what. We can get all that at home thank you very much.

Microchips With Everything

Whatever you buy these days seems to be computerised. They're even putting microchips into your wheelie bins now to keep an eye on what you're throwing away. Whatever next? Chips in your chips to make sure you don't eat too many?

And whoever thought you'd have microchips inside your pets?

Your dog has a microchip so he doesn't get lost. Your cat has a microchip so she's allowed in through your super duper state of the art cat flap.

Perhaps even your goldfish will have a chip soon. Or in other words – fish and chips.

Then there are phones. If you'd told Alexander Graham Bell that one day you'd be using your phone to take photos with he'd have had you locked up.

Nothing's simple any more. You try going to a phone shop and asking for a phone that you can just make and receive phone calls with and they'll look at you as if you're a fruit cake.

They say that before long your washing machine will have a chip in it which phones the manufacturer itself when it breaks down to call out a repair man. But you know what? They'll still say that the repair man will come 'any time between 8am and 6pm' next Tuesday, and you'll wait in all day, and the buggers still won't turn up.

No, progress is all very well, but we wrinklies prefer our chips with salt and vinegar thank you very much.

Original Things To Moan About Tomorrow

The wrinkly has certain subjects which he or she is duty bound to moan about: the weather, young people, bewildering modern technology, bad manners, modern 'art', incorrect use of the English language, slovenly dress, swearing, etc etc.

When two or three wrinklies are gathered together the subjects for discussion will more often include one, or possibly all, of the above. But! To keep life interesting and to avoid boring the XL pants off your wrinkly friends, perhaps it is time to think of something original to moan about.

SETI

Or the Search for Extra Terrestrial Intelligence. For the past goodness knows how many years scientists have been scouring the airwaves of the universe looking for aliens. As all wrinklies know, the aliens have been smuggling themselves into the country on containers without being spotted. What a colossal waste of money!

Five Boys Chocolate bars

Desperation, pacification, expectation, acclamation and realisation. If you're not a wrinkly you will have no idea what any of the above is about, but why oh why oh why can't you buy this wonderful chocolate bar anymore?

The Hadron Super Collider

If you had to invent a sure-fire way of wasting taxpayers' money you couldn't do much better than this: a vast machine lodged under the Swiss Alps or somewhere, firing particles around to see what happens. They might as well be firing £50 notes around, or just building a giant bonfire of them. Madness!

Floral clocks

Once upon a time many a trip to the seaside would be enlivened by the serendipitous discovery of a floral clock. Where are they all now? Gone digital we suppose.

Tectonic plates

Fancy building countries on top of tectonic plates! No wonder we have all these earthquakes and volcanoes and things. It's like building your house on a pile of Pontefract cakes with minds of their own.

Elephants

You go to a zoo, you expect zoo animals. Any fool can open an insect house in their spare room, but you try finding an elephant at London Zoo – you've got more chance of seeing a policeman!

Human statues

Now you don't mind slinging a few coppers into the hat of someone who can dance or sing (as long as it isn't Streets of London again), but some of these jokers expect you to stump up for watching them standing there doing nothing. Scandalous!

Fibonacci numbers

And any of that other mathematical stuff that ordinary people don't understand. So, you get a Fibonacci number by adding together the previous two. So what? Let's invent a new one: you get a Wrinklati number by adding together the previous three: 0, 1, 1, 2, 4, 7, 13, 24, 44... now can we have a Nobel prize?

Songs To Help Wrinklies Through The Day

Pop music is of course made for young people, and those old records from your youth were made for young people too. That means that there are precious few songs out there for the wrinkly. We have therefore suggested a few slight adaptations of classic songs for you to sing as you dance round your dining room, leap about in your lounge or boogie in the bedroom.

'Wrinkly The Best' – Tina Turner

'Olden Years' – David Bowie

'Stairlift to Paradise' – George Gershwin

'I Want Your Specs' – George Michael

'Take the Werthers With You' – Crowded House

'Walking Frame In Memphis' – Marc Cohn

'The Not So Young Ones' – Cliff Richard

'I Can't Get No Sanatogen' – Rolling Stones

'Give Me Sheltered Accommodation' – Rolling Stones

'My Degeneration' – The Who

'Denture the One That I Want' – John Travolta & Olivia Newton-John

'Freedom Pass' – Wham

'Beyond the Se-nile' – Bobby Darin

'Magic Carpet Slippers' – Mighty Dub Katz

'Middle-aged Spread Your Wings' – Queen

'I Bet You Look Good on the Darts Night' – Arctic Monkeys

'Get Ur Free Prescription' – Missy Elliott

'Can't Get Out Of My Bed' – Kylie Minogue

'I Predict a Riot Of Colour from My Spring Plantings' – Kaiser Chiefs

'Chasing Sidecars' – Snow Patrol

'I've Got Flu Babe' – Sonny & Cher

'A Lighter Shade of Ale' – Procol Harum

'Sad Gran's Disco' – Scott McKenzie

'Money's Too Tight in My Pension' – Simply Red

Headlines That Wrinklies Would Like To See In Their Morning Paper

Doctors Find Miracle Cure To Combat Ageing

Read all about it! Yes, you can roll back the years and look as young as some of those film stars who are actually older than you but look 30 years younger.

State Pension To Be Quadrupled

Well, even quadrupling it wouldn't mean it was a king's ransom but it would be a start.

Loud Car Stereo Systems To Be Outlawed

Them and piped music in shops and pubs, those irritating 'personal stereos', telephone 'hold' music and all the other so-called music you have to put up with all flipping day long.

Wrinkly Conquers Everest

Well, we need role models too you know. Surely it must be possible to build a stairlift up the north face somewhere.

A Wrinkly Page Three Model

If only to remind us that we're not the only people in the world with saggy bits.

The TV Guide In Large Print

By the time you've scoured through the tiny print with your magnifying glass and found out what time the Inspector Morse repeat is on he's already worked out whodunnit.

New Prime Minister Is Over 50!

If politicians get any younger they'll be sitting on high chairs in the House of Commons. Bring back politicians with grey hair and a bit of gravitas (even though Harold Wilson was only in his forties when he became PM and William Pitt the Younger was barely out of his teens.

Doctors Perfect Bladder Transplants

No more stumbling around in the middle of the night trying to get to the loo.

Public Hangings For Greedy Bankers

Well, let's face it, that would put a spring in anyone's step wouldn't it?

Automatic Custodial Sentences For Anyone Heard Swearing In A Public Place

About blooming time and all!

Are You Really A Wrinkly?

Statistically, you are quite likely to have received this book as a gift. There you were on your sixtieth (or perhaps even your fiftieth) birthday hoping for a present that would reflect your venerable status with its quiet dignity and good taste. Oh well...

So, somebody decided that you are now officially a wrinkly – but are you? Take this simple test to find out.

It's 10 o'clock in the evening, are you:
a)   Still out and about, completely oblivious to the time?
b)   Nodding off in front of the TV news?
c)   Tucked up in bed in your jimjams?

Do you wear:
a)   Designer clothes?
b)   Chain store clothes?
c)   It's so long since you last bought any clothes you can't remember where you got them?

Does the word 'apple' conjure up images of:
a)   A computer
b)   The Beatles' record label
c)   A nice pie with custard?

Is your pension something that you:
a)   Never think about?
b)   Have started to worry about?
c)   Try not to think about?

Do you drive:

a) A fast sports car?
b) A sensible, safe, and fuel-efficient car?
c) You're not allowed to drive anything any more

Are you:

a) Struggling to pay your mortgage?
b) Just paying off your mortgage?
c) Selling your house to pay for nursing care?

Do you:

a) Zip up the stairs two at a time?
b) Walk up the stairs carefully?
c) Zip up the stairs at the push of a button?

Answers

Mostly a's: You have no right to be reading this book! Swap it for The Clubber's Guide to the UK or keep it under lock and key until you've got past the 'mature' stage and started to go rotten.

Mostly b's: You're a borderline case. Will you teeter over into full wrinklyhood or draw back just at the last moment and grow old disgracefully?

Mostly c's: Nice to have you on board! Yes, you have passed the test with flying (well, shuffling) colours. Award yourself the WBE (Wrinkly of the British Empire) medal.

Positive Thoughts For Grumpy Wrinklies About Tomorrow

- Look on the bright side! Tomorrow is going to be better than today! And if it isn't, look on the bright side! Today was a better day than tomorrow's going to be!
- Tomorrow is a new day! They keep sending them because you complained so much about the old one!
- Look forward to tomorrow! Surely those around you must have run out of new ways to annoy you by now!
- Good things come to those who wait although by your age it might be worth checking you're standing in the right queue.
- Tomorrow is a day of wonderful opportunities. It will bring a vast, fresh array of incredible new experiences for you to moan about!
- The good thing about tomorrow is seeing a lot of people's confident predictions proved completely wrong!
- Tomorrow is the day when you can enjoy looking back nostalgically on the rotten time you've had today.
- Every day you get older makes each individual day a smaller and smaller percentage of your life! So by that way of thinking you're getting slightly less old each day!
- Tomorrow won't be so bad. And if it is, you should be getting used to it by now!
- You've waited a long time but eventually there's got to be a day when things go according to plan.

(Grumbling) Appendix

How To Speak Wrinkly

If you are new to the wrinkly world, or perhaps you are an unwrinkly having a sneaky look at this book before you give it to someone else you may like to be au fait with a few wrinkly terms. Here goes…

- 'Youngster' – Anyone under the age of 50.
- 'Old person' – Anyone five minutes or more older than you are.
- 'A bit of peace and quiet' – An unearthly silence akin to sudden deafness.
- 'A nice cup of tea' – One made by somebody else.
- 'Feeling a bit peaky' – Call an ambulance!
- 'Godawful racket' – Someone else's taste in music.
- 'Typical!' – Something has gone wrong as usual. Strangely never used when something has gone right.
- 'Forty winks' – A two-hour daytime kip with mouth gaping open like the Mersey tunnel and a snore like a startled buffalo.
- 'A bit of what you fancy' – A lot of what you fancy in an orgy of self-indulgence and potential damage to one's vital organs.
- 'Proper music' – Something with a tune, and words that can be easily distinguished (i.e. anything released before 1970).

- 'A bit of a knees-up' – An embarrassing display of terpsichorean abandon after 'a bit of what you fancy'.
- 'A bit parky' – The temperature has dropped to a level that would make an Everest climber's nose drop off.
- 'Decent TV programme' – One with no sex, no swearing, no violence, and not too many people under the age of 50 in it.
- 'Mustn't grumble'/ 'Could be worse'/ 'Surviving' – The wrinkly's choice of responses to the enquiry 'How are you?'
- 'Incredibly expensive' – The price of everything.
- 'A bargain' – Something that isn't really needed and which will soon be put up in the attic for all eternity.
- 'Rather complicated' – The wrinkly's assessment of any technical device introduced since 1973.
- 'It didn't seem to agree with me' – The meal you have just served me was inedible muck which almost killed me .
- 'Very nice I'm sure' – It was really horrible.
- 'Very interesting' – Of no interest to me whatsoever.
- 'I've heard you've not been too good recently' – I heard you were dead.
- 'Lovely weather' – It isn't raining.
- 'Terrible weather' – It is raining.

Glossary

There are certain words and phrases used in this book and elsewhere in the wrinklyverse (ah, there we are, there's another one) which may not be easily understandable by the public at large. So to assist in your enjoyment of this book we have provided a short glossary as follows:

Bingo wings

There is a tale (probably apocryphal) of one old dear who tried to order these from her local Chinese takeaway, but no, bingo wings are the unsightly appendages of excess flesh that hang heavily from under the arms when one's pencil is hovering expectantly over one's bingo card.

Dalek years (the)

The point in a wrinkly's life when they are no longer able to get up the stairs.

Gazunder

Nothing to do with gazumping, the gazunder is the wrinklies' chamberpot of choice because it 'goes under' the bed.

Grubes

Intimate body hair that has turned grey leaving the area between a wrinkly's legs looking a bit like Tom Jones now he's stopped using Grecian 2000.

Moobs

A slightly quicker way of referring to your man boobs.

Muffin top

The ridge of fat spilling up and over the top of your pants is said to make you look a bit like a muffin. Well, as they say, you are what you eat.

Pharmaceutical advent calendar

Plastic box which organises all your pills and medication according to which day you must take them.

Silver surfers

Wrinklies who have discovered the internet and have thus somehow become associated with a Marvel Comics superhero in the process although the original Silver Surfer probably didn't spend quite so much time researching his family tree and sending emails to his children in Australia.

Sognobs

Biscuits that have been too liberally dunked in tea.

Wind tunnel effect

Not a reference to any sort of bowel disorder but the look achieved by wrinklies who have had a bit of cosmetic surgery. The wind tunnel is clearly going to get you at one end or the other.

Wrinkleati

Readers will be familiar with such terms as literati, glitterati and twitterati, meaning the cream of the worlds of literature, showbiz, and twits. The wrinkleati is of course our equivalent.

Good Night, Wrinklies

It's time to say good night, sweet wrinklies. Time to go up the wooden hill to Bedfordshire and slip away into the deep dark wrinkle of sleep.

However if reading this book still hasn't left you ready to drop off – although goodness knows, we've tried our best – then please take advantage of the additional sleep-inducing element contained in the volume.

Yes, this book has been sprinkled with magic wrinkly sleepy dust. Shake the book over your pillow before bedtime to release the magic sleepy dust and you should soon fall into a deep relaxing sleep (albeit after several minutes continuous sneezing from the cloud of dust now hanging over your headboard).

If this still doesn't make you drowsy, shake the book even more vigorously for about half an hour. You should then collapse sweating and exhausted into bed and, thanks to magic wrinkly sleepy dust, fall swiftly asleep.

If you're still not feeling tired, what in heaven's name have you been taking? Clearly you will need an elephant tranquilliser to get off to sleep.

You could try battering yourself insensible with the book. Your wrinkly partner might like to assist with this process particularly after all the time you've been keeping them awake. And also this should release an enormous amount of magic wrinkly sleepy dust at the same time.

Or you could just read the entire book again from the start. Well, your wrinkly memory will probably have forgotten most of it by now!

Night night!